No one knew for sure how she died. They only found small pricks on her arm. Some said she brought an asp to her…

Dio Cassius,
Roman History,
2d–3d century CE

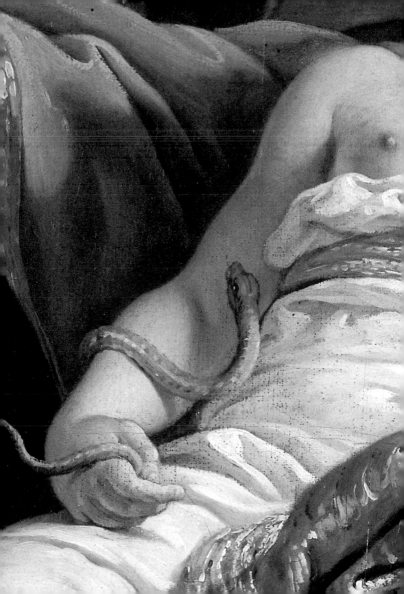

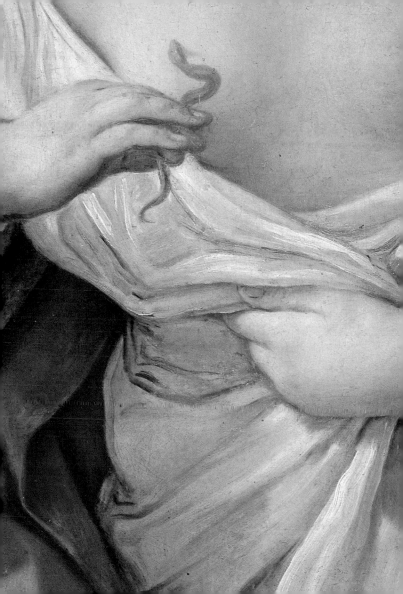

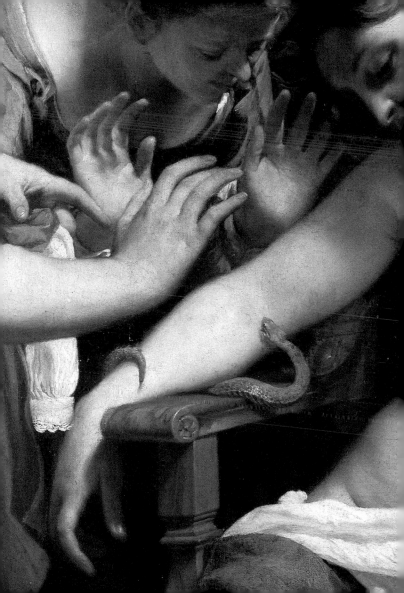

CONTENTS

CLEOPATRA
THE LIFE AND DEATH
OF A PHARAOH

Edith Flamarion

DISCOVERIES®

HARRY N. ABRAMS, INC., PUBLISHERS

Plutarch tells us ("Life of Alexander," 1st–2d century CE) that in 331 BCE, Alexander had conquered Egypt and was planning to settle a colony of Greeks there, he resolved to build a large and populous city, and give it his own name. The baby girl born in Alexandria during the winter of 69–68 BCE in the luxurious apartments of the concubine of the pharaoh Ptolemy XII was given the Greek name Cleopatra. She was descended from the long line of Macedonian rulers, known as the Ptolemies, who had reigned over the country since the death of the great conqueror.

CHAPTER 1

ALEXANDRIA, CITY OF THE LIGHTHOUSE

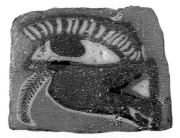

The Golden City, the City of the Lighthouse, Most Brilliant Alexandria—the Ancients devised innumerable praise-names for this Egyptian city, whose renown and splendor reached their zenith during Cleopatra's reign. Left: the lighthouse as imagined in a drawing of 1725. Right: Alexandrian glasswork.

In 304 BCE Cleopatra's ancestor, Ptolemy I Soter ("the Savior"), founded the dynasty of the Ptolemies. He was a Macedonian, one of the *diadochoi,* or successors of the conquerer Alexander the Great, and had been a general in his army. Six princesses before her were called Cleopatra, whose name means "her father's glory." Thus the baby's heritage was Greek, though there were "barbarians," or non-Greeks, in her lineage. Her great-grandmother was one of the king of Syria's daughters, a Seleucid with Persian blood.

The family soon included another baby girl, Arsinoë, and two boys, the future Ptolemy XIII and Ptolemy XIV. There was nothing cozy about this family: like those on the throne before them, they were torn by intrigues, ambition, and jealousy. The women were as active as the men, since Egyptian pharaonic law, which the Ptolemies perpetuated, allowed a woman to ascend to the glorious throne. A ruling queen was the spouse of her brother and co-ruler, for the pharaonic couple was by tradition the deceased pharaoh's wedded eldest son and daughter. Two potential rivals stood between Cleopatra and the succession: Berenice and Cleopatra VI, the daughters of Ptolemy XII's first wife and sister, Cleopatra, known as Tryphaeana, "the Pleasure-Seeker."

The Ptolemies valued their Macedonian heritage; despite the African and Asian influences of the country they governed, they lived in the Greek manner,

At his death in 283 BCE, Ptolemy I (left, on a 4th-century BCE coin) left behind a very prosperous kingdom. When the body of Alexander the Great was brought back to Alexandria, the city became the true capital of Egypt.

Tombs

Harbor
Good Re

Necropolis

RHA

Cana

Sta

Hypog
(Catac

LAKE
MAREO

dressed in the Greek way, spoke Greek—the *koine,* or language common to all the Hellenistic realms—and worshiped Greek gods, who they attempted to identify with local divinities. As

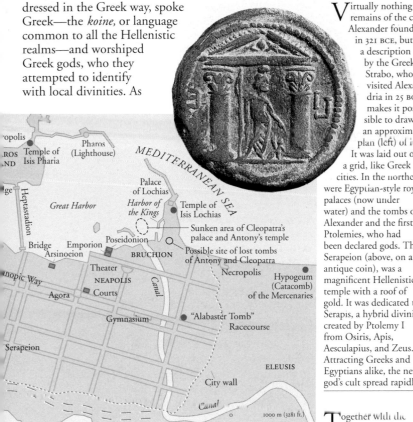

Virtually nothing remains of the city Alexander founded in 321 BCE, but a description by the Greek Strabo, who visited Alexandria in 25 BCE, makes it possible to draw an approximate plan (left) of it. It was laid out on a grid, like Greek cities. In the northeast were Egyptian-style royal palaces (now under water) and the tombs of Alexander and the first Ptolemies, who had been declared gods. The Serapeion (above, on an antique coin), was a magnificent Hellenistic temple with a roof of gold. It was dedicated to Serapis, a hybrid divinity created by Ptolemy I from Osiris, Apis, Aesculapius, and Zeus. Attracting Greeks and Egyptians alike, the new god's cult spread rapidly.

Together with the Ptolemaic rulers, their wives, mistresses, sisters, and mothers— many named Arsinoë, Berenice, Cleopatra— engaged in royal power plays, court intrigues, and sometimes deadly plots. Far left: the portrait of a Ptolemaic queen, mid-2d century BCE.

the geographer Strabo wrote in the 1st century BCE: They were "mindful of the customs common to the Greeks."

Brilliant Alexandria

The city in which Cleopatra was born was, at the time, the largest of the ancient world. This proud metropolis was a far cry from the little seacoast village of Ra-Kedet (in Greek, Rhakotis) where Alexander had chosen in 331 BCE to found a Mediterranean port, to which he gave his name—as he did with the seventy other cities he created. Plutarch tells us that the site was indicated to Alexander in his sleep by "a gray-headed old man of venerable aspect."

The new city was at the crossroads of Europe, Asia, and Africa. It was perfectly situated near the western mouth of the Nile delta, protected on the east by the great river, on the north by the little island of Pharos, and on the south by Lake Mareotis. Ptolemy I made it the capital of Egypt, rather than the important ancient city of Thebes, which was too far from the sea and was in the hands of the Egyptian high priests. (Cairo, which was to become a great city a thousand years later, was at this time a nameless village.)

In Cleopatra's time Alexandria was at the height of its magnificence, with splendid marble monuments, palaces, theaters, amphitheaters, and temples. Chief among these were temples to Poseidon and Dionysus, patron gods of the Ptolemies, and the Serapeion, or temple of Serapis, a god introduced into Egypt by the Ptolemies as a fusion of Greek Zeus and Aesculapius and Egyptian Apis and Osiris.

The island of Pharos boasted one of the Seven Wonders of the World: a resplendent marble lighthouse tower, 423 feet high (130 m), whose elegance and proportions stirred the admiration of the ancients. Built under

The Ptolemies were skillful politicians: in pairing Serapis with the ancestral Egyptian goddess Isis (left, on a 2d-century CE sculpture), Healer, Protector of Sailors, Leader of the Muses, Goddess of Ten Thousand Names, they linked traditional religion with the newer Greek religion.

Ptolemy II by the Cnidian architect Sostratus to guide ships into port, it had a powerful fire at the summit, visible at sea to a distance of over 30 miles (50 km).

Cleopatra lived in the northeast quarter of the city, the Bruchion. This impressive complex of royal palaces and gardens ran along the seafront in an area that vanished under water when the coastline shifted in later centuries. The city of Alexandria, a grid of wide avenues about 3¾ miles (6 km) long and 1 mile (1.6 km) wide, hugging the Mediterranean coast, had been laid out by Dinocrates of Rhodes. A broad causeway connected the island of Pharos to the mainland. This was called the Heptastadion, for it was seven *stadia,* or about 1,300 yards (1,200 m) in length; it divided two ports: the Great Harbor to the east, across from the Bruchion, and the Harbor of Good Return to the west. The ancient causeway has since silted up, so that the island of Pharos is now a promontory.

"The greatest emporium in the inhabited world"

The streets teemed with a very dense population: three hundred thousand Alexandrians lived in the city itself, seven hundred thousand in the greater metropolitan area. They were a cosmopolitan mix, made up essentially of three large groups: the Greek community, which lived in the center of town; the Jewish

Charming terra-cotta figurines were exported from Alexandria throughout the Mediterranean in the Hellenistic period.

❝The extremity of the isle is a rock, which…has upon it a tower that is admirably constructed of white marble with many stories," wrote Strabo in the 1st-century BCE *Geography.* The Lighthouse (left, in a modern reconstruction) was surmounted by a colossal statue, probably of Zeus the Savior. It was still standing in the 14th century, when it was damaged by an earthquake. Later, the Mameluk Quait Bey used its fallen stones to build a fort on the same site.

community, in the eastern quarter; and the Egyptians—
the poorest group—in the old city in the western
quarter. Sailors, merchants, artisans, functionaries, and
mercenaries lived side by side.

The city was livable thanks to
an ingenious system of canals,
reservoirs, and filters that
purified the waters of the Nile
and Lake Mareotis. In hot
weather, when the gardens were
not enough to cool the desert
air, the Alexandrians moved to
the shores of Lake Mareotis,
where the richer citizens built
sumptuous country houses
amid vineyards, gardens,
and orchards.

The crossroads of the
caravan routes between
Africa and Asia (from India
and China) and of the great
sea routes, the city was a marketplace for countless
products—ivory, spices, exotic fruits, foodstuffs, wines,
and art objects—"the greatest emporium in the
inhabited world," as Strabo said. At the time,
Alexandria was also the most important grain port
of the Mediterranean. Wheat was stored in silos that
the Greek papyri called *thesauroi*, or treasuries.
Pleasures, too, were for sale: the outlying districts of
Eleusis and Canopus were known for their dancing
girls and boy prostitutes, the *cinaedi*.

Left: a Greco-Roman
terra-cotta lantern
in the shape of an
Alexandrian house.

Below and right: a
large mosaic in Italy,
most likely made by
Greek artists from Egypt
c. 100 BCE, depicts the
teeming life along the
Nile in Hellenized Egypt.
From left: a banquet
under a pergola; fisher-
men; *hoplites,* or Greek
soldiers, in front of what
may be the royal palace;
a peasant in front of his
home; a procession
to a small Greek temple;
and (above) Egyptian
sanctuaries with pylons.

The home of the Muses

Alexandria was also the locus of an intense intellectual and artistic life, though the great days of the "School of Alexandria" were long past, when, in the 3d century BCE, the mathematician Euclid, the poets Theocritus and Callimachus, and the painter Apelles had presided. The equally splendid Neo-Platonists were not to come for another two hundred years. But 1st-century BCE Alexandria still offered myriad seductions for the lover of knowledge.

Cultural life was concentrated in two buildings in the royal quarter: the Library and the Museum, both founded by Ptolemy I, who, like his successors, sponsored

The Nile, whose floods rise in early summer when the other rivers that feed the Mediterranean run dry, brought deposits of rich, fertile soil to Egypt.

the collection of manuscripts and documents. In Cleopatra's day, the Library numbered some seven hundred thousand works; this made it, with the library of Pergamum, the largest collection of books in the western world. Scribes copied, revised, and annotated the texts, and the science of philology made enormous progress.

The Museum—that is, a place dedicated to the Muses, who personified intellectual and artistic activity—was a center of scientific research.

Its great hall, suitable for meetings and conferences; its arcaded walks and vast dining room all facilitated exchanges between scholars, who received royal subsidies so that they might devote their time to study. This was the age of methodology and taxonomy: the scholars of Alexandria invented systems of record-keeping and of classification; they compiled erudite lists, and it is thanks to their formidable labors that many ancient texts have come down to us. The museum was a great cradle of the modern sciences, of rhetoric, philosophy, medicine, anatomy, geometry, hydrostatics, geography, and astronomy.

The art, literature and learning of Alexandria greatly influenced Rome, the other pole of the Mediterranean basin. The Roman poets Catullus, Propertius, Ovid, and others drew inspiration from the Egyptian fountainhead, and the Romans indulged a taste for the refined arts of the city; they were particularly fond of the gold jewelry set with precious stones and the chased-silver plate that

Around 290 BCE, Demetrius, an Athenian at the court of Ptolemy I, founded the Museum, a research center under the protection of the Muses that attracted the greatest scholars of the day. The Library, probably at first just an annex, was directed by learned men such as Zenodotus, the first editor of Homer; Callimachus, who organized its catalogue; and the geographer Eratosthenes. In Cleopatra's time, the Library contained 700 *volumina,* scrolls of papyrus (above) rolled around a dowel; these were indexed, labeled, and organized on shelves. All the contemporary spheres of knowledge were represented—including treatises on pastry. A branch Library was later established in the Serapeion. Far left: a 4th-century BCE Ptolemaic statue; right: a 19th-century re-creation of the Library.

were Alexandrian specialties. The statuettes that flooded the Mediterranean rim convey the Alexandrian taste for exaggerated realism, for the bizarre, the grotesque, even the deformed, while the houses of Pompeii preserved the painting style that was admired in Egypt.

Egypt, a tempting prey for Rome

In a vast enterprise of conquest, Rome gradually took over most of the countries on the coast of the Mediterranean, which it would soon call *mare nostrum*—"our sea." In the 1st century BCE, the Egyptian bloc was one of the most important to remain independent; to the Romans it represented the gateway to Africa and Asia, as well as being a major economic and military prize in itself.

Egypt was the wealthiest of the Hellenistic (late-classical Greek) states. The Ptolemaic realm was a staggering prosperity machine whose riches, by and large, went to the country's rulers. Its planned economy was for the most part controlled by the Greeks, who comprised one fifth of the population of seven million inhabitants. Land use was strictly codified and supervised by civil servants (*nomarchs, toparchs,* and secretaries) who answered to the Greek *strategus,* an all-powerful

"For by nature the land produces more fruit than do other lands, and still more when watered… but diligence has oftentimes, even when nature has failed, availed to bring about the watering of…land."

Strabo, *Geography,*
1st century BCE

Much of the wealth of the Ptolemaic state derived from agriculture. The land belonged to the pharaohs, the priests, and Greek colonists but was cultivated by the indigenous people, who were burdened with rents and taxes.

Egyptian-inspired works of art have been found in Rome; one example is this precious cup (left) discovered near Naples. Of obsidian inlaid with enamels and gold wire, it is decorated with a scene of offerings made to the goddess Hathor, in the form of a cow with a solar disk, and to Horus, symbolized by a hawk.

official in charge of one of several administrative units. Agricultural techniques and crops imported by Greek military colonists (the *cleruchs*) resulted in an improved use of the soil. The rich area of Fayum, for example, was cultivated by a strong Greek colony.

The state controlled all production: it held monopolies on oil, beer, papyrus, and flax, and imposed a burdensome system of contracts and licenses on private businesses. The royal workshops were closely supervised. Prices were set regardless of manufacturing costs. The Ptolemaic state produced much, consumed little, and exported a great deal. In the storehouses of Alexandria enormous quantities of goods were amassed to be sent abroad. All these revenues were managed by a great number of banks, the most powerful of which belonged to the state and were practically public coffers, receiving taxes, duties, and licensing fees and multiplying their value through investments and loans. The Ptolemies devised an innovative system in which bankers were personally responsible for the assets they managed. Revenues poured into the vast royal treasury, allowing the pharaoh to support a strong army—useful in maintaining control of a country constantly menaced from within by nationalist movements and religious opposition, and from outside by Rome, Persia, and other neighbors.

Rome had long desired Egypt's gold. At every conflict, internal or external, the Romans stepped in as arbitrators, on occasion with an iron fist; while Egypt played the Roman card in its dealings with the immense Asian kingdom of the Seleucids.

Left: oxen turning a mill or pump, from a 1st-century BCE tomb fresco at Sakkieh.

A network of administrators managed the country (below, a statue of the governor of Tanis, late Ptolemaic period). At the top of the hierarchy, in Alexandria, the *dioicetus,* a sort of prime minister, oversaw the collection of taxes, in cash and in kind, that poured into the royal coffers and storehouses. Frequent correspondence kept all the pharaoh's representatives in close contact.

The flute-playing pharaoh

In 80 BCE, Sulla, dictator of the Roman Republic, intervened diplomatically to force the queen of Egypt, Cleopatra-Berenice, to marry her nephew, Ptolemy XI. It was a melancholy marriage, indeed, for it ended some months later with the assassination of the pharaoh—after he had ordered his wife killed. The throne in Alexandria was next occupied by a natural son of Ptolemy X. This new pharaoh, Ptolemy XII, was our Cleopatra's father. He took on the prestigious epithets of Neos Dionysus ("new Dionysus"), Philopator ("he who loves his father"), and Philometor ("he who loves his mother")— but the people soon nicknamed him Auletes, "the Flute-Player."

He had a notorious taste for parties and banquets, where he was given to drinking heavily and playing music among the dancing girls. Revolts by farmers and the indigenous population, economic problems, and deterioration of the nation's finances began to tear the country apart; the pharaoh, virtually ignored these problems, allowed corruption to flourish. Furthermore, Auletes lived in terror of losing his throne, a fear the Romans exploited by repeatedly claiming that there

Left: This exquisite carved bowl (2d–1st century BCE) is a perfect example of the dynastic propaganda that proclaimed the prosperity of the country under the Ptolemies. In it are blended Egyptian and Greek sculptural styles: Isis-Cleopatra reclines with her arm on the sphinx of Osiris; both figures are Egyptian, while the Nile, personified as an old man holding a cornucopia, is in the Alexandrian style, as are the standing figure of the child heir Horus-Triptolemus and the Seasons, at right, reminiscent of the three Graces.

existed a will drafted by Ptolemy XI, according to which the late sovereign had bequeathed Egypt to Rome. The Roman Senate, referring to this alleged will, had seized the late pharaoh's personal

possessions, but for its own political reasons it favored Egypt's continuing autonomy. In 65 BCE and again in 64 BCE the Senate, supported by the aristocracy, opposed proposals to reduce Egypt to a Roman province, no doubt fearing that the powerful men behind the idea, such as Caesar and Crassus, would gain too much from the change.

Pompey the Great at the gates of Egypt

One man especially became the champion of Egyptian independence: the Roman *imperator* (commander) Pompey the Great, wreathed in glory after suppressing a revolt in Rome, clearing the Mediterranean of pirates, and crushing the powerful Asian king Mithradates. In 64 BCE he overthrew the Seleucid kingdom; the following year, he reduced Syria to the status of a Roman province—thereby creating a Roman stronghold in the

"[Auletes] apart from his general licentiousness, practised the accompaniment of choruses with the flute, and upon this he prided himself so much that he would not hesitate to celebrate contests in the royal palace, and at these contests would come forward to vie with the opposing contestants."
Strabo,
Geography,
1st century BCE

During the reign of Ptolemy XII Auletes (above and left), a ruler much vilified by some Alexandrians, Egypt fell into debt and became considerably weakened.

Middle East, at the gates of Egypt—and took Jerusalem. Auletes made an alliance with Pompey, sending him 8,000 cavalry for his wars and many gifts, among them a heavy gold crown.

In 60 BCE, though, the pharaoh had reason to tremble, for Pompey allied himself with Julius Caesar, who became consul the following year. The Egyptian king sent to Rome the huge sum of 8,000 talents, which bought him official acknowledgment of his authority. Julian law declared Ptolemy XII Auletes "an ally and friend of the Roman people," which made him, in reality, a vassal.

Yet danger was inching nearer. In 58 BCE Rome attacked Auletes' brother, who ruled Cyprus. He took poison, and his conqueror, Cato, seized the island and its treasury, which he turned over to the Senate.

Auletes driven from Alexandria

The looming military presence of Rome may have alarmed the Alexandrians, who rebelled against their ruler. Driven out by his subjects, Auletes fled Egypt for Rome. There, beginning in 57 BCE he launched a campaign of politicking and corruption, seeking to regain the throne of Egypt and to rally to his cause every powerful citizen of

In the middle of the 1st century BCE, Pompey the Great (left, a marble portrait) was the strong-man of the Roman East. His victories over the kingdoms of Pontus and Syria gave him control of the whole region. It was to his friend Gabinius, governor of Syria, that he gave the order to invade Egypt.

the Roman capital. Auletes bribed senators, spending so much that he was obliged to borrow from Rabirius, a wealthy Roman financier.

In the meantime, the Alexandrians put his eldest daughter, Berenice IV, on the throne, and sent a delegation to Rome to request the Senate to arbitrate

the conflict between father and daughter. While Rome hesitated, equivocated, and consulted sacred texts, Auletes simply arranged to have a number of the delegates assassinated. But Rome was reluctant to commit a large armed force to returning Auletes to power. In despair, the deposed pharaoh left Rome for Ephesus, in Asia Minor. Cleopatra, then about ten years old, remained in Alexandria, where her half-sister now reigned.

Rome takes up arms

It was then that Rome decided upon a miltary intervention. One of Pompey's lieutenants, Gabinius, governor of Syria, marched on Egypt at the head of a mighty army—an expedition in which the ten thousand talents promised by Auletes undoubtedly played a part. Leading the cavalry was a fiery twenty-four-year-old officer named Mark Antony. Gabinius took Pelusium, then Alexandria; Archilaus, Berenice's husband, died in combat. Auletes entered the Egyptian capital as its conqueror, and immediately had his daughter executed.

With the pharaoh back on his throne, Gabinius quit Egypt, leaving behind a military guard composed in the main of German and Gallic mercenaries. The Roman Rabirius, Auletes' creditor, became his prime minister in Egypt.

Rome's might and that of its overseas government rested on its soldiers (left and opposite, a statue of a legionnaire), true professionals in an immense standing army established at the end of the 2d century BCE. Hardened and well-trained, they were subjected to a rigorous discipline that placed them entirely under the authority of their Imperator, or general-in-chief, who had the *imperium*—power of life and death—over them. Besides Roman citizens, the army included Gallic, Numidian, Spanish, German, and Thracian mercenaries; despite its diversity, it was at the time one of the best in the world. The army of the Ptolemies, however effective its cadres of Greek fighters, was hard pressed to withstand Rome.

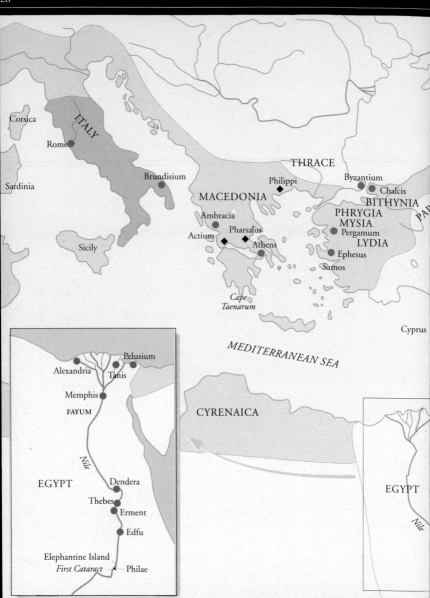

Corsica

ITALY

Rome

Sardinia

Brundisium

Sicily

THRACE

Philippi ◆

Byzantium

Chalcis

MACEDONIA

BITHYNIA

PHRYGIA

Ambracia

MYSIA

Actium ◆

Pharsalus ◆

Pergamum

LYDIA

Athens

Ephesus

Samos

PAR

Cape
Taenarum

Cyprus

MEDITERRANEAN SEA

Pelusium

Alexandria

Tanis

Memphis

FAYUM

CYRENAICA

EGYPT

Nile

Dendera

Thebes

Erment

Edfu

Elephantine Island
First Cataract ◄ Philae

EGYPT

Nile

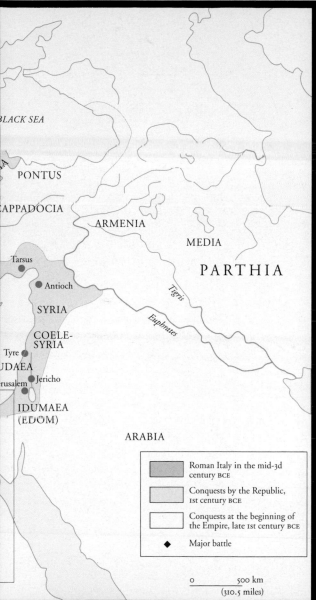

BLACK SEA

PONTUS

CAPPADOCIA

ARMENIA

MEDIA

PARTHIA

Tarsus

Antioch

Tigris

SYRIA

Euphrates

COELE-
SYRIA

Tyre

JUDAEA

Jericho

Jerusalem

IDUMAEA
(EDOM)

ARABIA

Roman Italy in the mid-3d
century BCE

Conquests by the Republic,
1st century BCE

Conquests at the beginning of
the Empire, late 1st century BCE

◆ Major battle

0   500 km
        (310.5 miles)

Beginning in the early 3d century BCE, Rome gradually conquered the area surrounding the Mediterranean basin. It was a vast empire, webbed by a network of sea and land routes and organized politically on the model of the Roman city. Magistrates risen through the ranks—proconsuls and propraetors, for the most part—governed provinces acquired by invasion or inheritance. The result was a heady mix of cultures deeply marked by Hellenism.

The eastern sector—far from Rome, divided into numerous states, and near the disruptive kingdom of Parthia—proved the most difficult to subdue. Yet by the middle of the 1st century BCE, most of the area—Pergamum, Bithynia, Pontus, Cilicia, Syria, and Cyprus—was in Roman hands. Only Judaea and Egypt were semiautonomous; their rulers, Herod and Cleopatra, were subject monarchs, placed and maintained in power by the Romans.

When Ptolemy XII Auletes died in 51 BCE, his will named as his successors his two eldest children: Cleopatra, who was eighteen years old, and Ptolemy XIII, who was ten, and whom she must marry, according to Ptolemaic dynastic law. This marriage in name only left her perfectly free to rule as she chose. She became Cleopatra VII, "mistress of the two lands," that is, reigning over Upper and Lower Egypt.

CHAPTER 2
AN EIGHTEEN-YEAR-OLD QUEEN

The two faces of Cleopatra: a descendant of Alexander the Great's general, the queen had herself portrayed (left) with the attributes of a pharaoh in the bas-reliefs of Egyptian temples and in the Greco-Roman style (right: a marble portrait bust).

As custom decreed, Cleopatra VII took a surname—Philopator, Greek for "she who loves her father." The immeasurable powers of the pharaohs were now concentrated in her hands: she was the "living law," guarantor of order and prosperity. Cleopatra, who literally owned her subjects as well as her territory, was a living goddess, wreathed in the cult of royalty, worshiped by Egyptian and Greek priests alike.

An educated woman

Cleopatra had passed her early childhood in the royal women's apartments. She was educated according to the centuries-old program established for the pharaoh's daughters, who were raised to rule alongside their brother-husbands—the girls' curriculum was, in fact, the same as the boys'. The pharaonic tradition had given a great deal of importance to scholarship, and the Ptolemies honored and even intensified this tradition. Like all the Hellenistic rulers, they sought to nurture the child's general culture, or *enkukléios paidéia*—the phrase from which we get the word "encyclopedia." The Ptolemies developed a nationwide system of primary and secondary schools, for the Greek elite of girls and boys who would be called upon to maintain the pharaoh's power over the native masses.

"Discussions for the philosophers, theaters for the poets, dance groups and concerts, well-run conversations around the banquet tables...."
The Axiochus, late 4th century BCE?

"There is no record in history of other people more musical than the Alexandrians."
Athenaeus, *The Deipnosophists*, Book IV, c. 200 CE

Left: a 2d-century BCE terra-cotta figurine of Attis, a Phrygian god, dancing.

In Cleopatra's time, the course of study was based on Greek literature, especially the works considered masterpieces, which scholars had painstakingly assembled into a fixed canon, or collection of texts.

Thus, the child read and studied Homer's epics, which were much admired at court; the poems of Hesiod and Pindar; the tragedies of Euripides, considered superior to those of Aeschylus and Sophocles; the comedies of Menander; and the *Histories* of Herodotus and Thucydides; Cleopatra learned the art of rhetoric from the speeches of Demosthenes. Her education in the sciences was equally thorough: she took courses in arithmetic and geometry, astronomy and medicine, disciplines that flourished in the Alexandrian schools. A gifted amateur, the young queen also learned to draw, play the seven-stringed lyre, and sing. She was an excellent horsewoman—a sure sign of Hellenism in a "barbarian" land.

Her intellectual abilities were remarkable, but the queen displayed a particular talent for foreign languages,

Egyptian papyri, tablets, and *ostraca* from the Hellenistic period (above: a 2d-century BCE papyrus on astronomy) testify to the country's rich intellectual life and to the continuity of its educational system since the time of Alexander. The curriculum was very well-rounded, aiming to develop the individual morally, intellectually, and physically; it also preserved the Greek character of the governing elite. Literature, rhetoric, medicine, and astronomy were the subjects most studied, along with mathematics, which included music.

though Plutarch may have exaggerated somewhat when he wrote: "It was a pleasure merely to hear the sound of her voice, with which, like an instrument of many strings, she could pass from one language to another; so that there were few of the barbarian nations that she answered by an interpreter; to most of them she spoke herself, as to the Aethiopians, Troglodytes, Hebrews, Arabians, Syrians, Medes, Parthians, and many others, whose language she had learnt." She was one of the few members of her family who spoke these languages fluently, thus facilitating diplomatic negotiations.

She displayed a great natural bent for the sciences, which may be why Photinus, a master of arithmetic and geometry, titled his work *Cleopatra's Canon*. When she was still very young, she surrounded herself with persons of great learning, such as the physician Dioscorides and the astronomer Sosigenes, who later recast the calendar at Julius Caesar's behest. Cleopatra's intelligence, inquisitive spirit, and pleasure in intellectual matters were highlighted by a marked, sometimes almost overbearing sense of humor. Yet this queen who loved puns and jokes was developing, beneath a playful temperament, a fierce energy and tenacious will.

More than a pretty face

Was she only beautiful? To the historian Dio Cassius, fervent though he was in singing the praises of Cleopatra's enemy Octavian (Augustus), she was peerlessly beautiful, and in this lay her irresistible charm. She was "brilliant to look upon and to listen to, with the power to

Schoolchildren read, copied, and summarized the Greek authors, especially Homer (Alexander was said to have carried his copy of the *Iliad* with him everywhere). Left: a figurine of a young student.

Cleopatra is said to have written a treatise on cosmetics. Alexandrian women used perfume and loved unguents, scented oils, and eye makeup (below: making perfume, from a late-Ptolemaic relief).

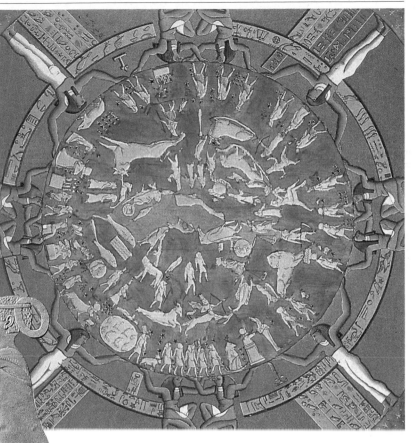

subjugate every one, even [Julius Caesar,] a
love-sated man already past his prime."
Plutarch was more moderate: "Her actual
beauty…was not in itself so remarkable that
none could be compared with her, or that
no one could see her without being struck by
it." The latter is more in keeping with the
portraits of her that have been found.

In any case, Cleopatra enchanted those who
saw her. "[The] contact of her presence,…was
irresistible"—Plutarch again—"the attraction

This circular depiction
of a section of the
heavens, dating from
Cleopatra's time, shows
the planets, constellations,
and decans and signs of
the zodiac. During the
Ptolemaic era, astronomy
was often used for
astrological purposes.

of her person, joining with the charm of her conversation, and the character that attended all she said or did, was something bewitching." When she spoke, "her grace in conversation, the sweetness and kindness of her nature, seasoned everything she said or did." Dio Cassius agreed: "She also possessed a most charming voice and a knowledge of how to make herself agreeable to every one." Her seductiveness, the ancients tell us, lay not only in her voice, but in her vivacity and intelligence. However, she also knew how to make the most of clothing, perfumes, and jewels. The women of Alexandria were famous for the artfulness of their cosmetics, their complicated coiffures, and their rich purple robes. On feast days they wore immaculate white garments, adorned with chased brooches and bracelets, gold pins, and pearl earrings and necklaces.

Fully a queen

Like her forebears, Cleopatra ruled by edicts, orders, and instructions, aided by a staff of courtiers, "friends," and "relatives." Assisted by the *dioicetus* (prime minister), she supervised the functionaries and Greek *strategoi* in charge of the districts of the territory. At the same time, as pharaoh, she had to be accessible to the public, receiving petitions and

> "Cleopatra's nose, had it been shorter, the whole face of the world would have been changed."
>
> Pascal

Cleopatra has come to epitomize feminine seductiveness, but her profile, as busts and medallions show, was strong and full of character (left and opposite). For the rest, we can only imagine what gave her the charm the ancients unanimously acknowledged: no full-length statue of her survives, nor does any contemporary text give a specific physical description of her. Her attractions were many: "It was a pleasure merely to hear the sound of her voice," says Plutarch. She enjoyed wearing precious jewels, and adored pearls, as did Caesar. Below: Cleopatra's name in Greek.

ΚΛΕ

requests in her own hands, dispensing justice in person. The task was a demanding one, fraught with difficulties. The vast Egyptian bureaucracy was paralyzing the country; among the indigenous peoples nationalism was rumbling; the peasants, ravaged by severe famines in 50 and 49 BCE, were rebeling, swelling the numbers of bandits that devastated the countryside; the Egyptian currency had weakened significantly; and above all the country had grown increasingly

The serpent is at the heart of Cleopatra's story: an attribute of Isis, the snake adorned the pharaohs' diadem. Later identified with the Bible's evil snake, this emblem associated Cleopatra with Eve. Left: a gold Roman bracelet, 1st century CE.

dependent on Rome. These problems were aggravated by the hostility brewing toward the young queen within her own circle. Her youngest sister, Arsinoë, coveted the throne, while her brother-husband was being manipulated by three advisors anatagonistic to her: the eunuch Photinus, the soldier Achillas, and the rhetorician Theodotus.

Cleopatra soon proved her political genius, quickly imposing the measures she

deemed necessary. She devalued the currency by a third in order to increase the exports that were indispensable to the Egyptian economy and launched a program of forced loans. She also engaged in a new religious policy, calculated to attract both the indigenous peoples and the all-powerful priestly class, who owned much of the land. Chiefly, however, Cleopatra addressed her country's foreign affairs. She was determined to avoid war with Rome, whose troops were stationed throughout the Middle East. When two sons of Bibulus, the Roman proconsul of Syria, were assassinated in Alexandria in 50 BCE, Cleopatra delivered the alleged killers to the proconsul as evidence of her goodwill. She then offered Pompey her support in his rivalry with Julius Caesar for control of Rome. Pompey, traditionally an ally of the Ptolemies, seemed at this time the stronger contender, though Caesar, beginning a civil war by crossing the Rubicon River in Italy with a rebel army, had driven him out of Rome in 49 BCE. Cleopatra now sent Pompey soldiers and provisions (there was a rumor at the time that she had had an affair with his young son, Cnaeus Pompeius, when he came as an envoy to Alexandria). Cleopatra's official support of Pompey provoked the Alexandrians' anger, but it was Ptolemy and Arsinoë's intrigues that fostered a revolt against her. In early 48 BCE Cleopatra was forced to flee the capital and seek refuge among the Arab tribes east of Egypt's border, near Syria.

The queen promptly attempted to take back her realm without outside reinforcements. She

"Isis the Great...who gives life..., the powerful ruler of the gods, whose name is raised above the goddesses..., without whom no one may enter the palace...."

Ptolemaic inscription from the Temple of Isis at Philae

In the era of the Ptolemies, Isis became a universal goddess, with whom Cleopatra, "the New Isis," was identified. The Ptolemies built a number of shrines to her, enclosing statues dressed in the traditional style. Left: a late-Ptolemaic Isis figure.

raised an army of
mercenaries but was
stopped at Mount Casius,
at the eastern mouth of
the Nile near Pelusium, by
the young king's troops,
commanded by his three
regents. The two armies
would have clashed had
not Pompey arrived
unexpectedly on 28 September 48 BCE, in the aftermath
of his crushing defeat by Caesar's troops at Pharsalus,
in Greece.

"Dead men don't bite": the death of Pompey

The defeated Imperator, after wandering for forty days
about the Mediterranean, hunted by Caesar, resolved
finally to seek asylum with Auletes' children—a grave
miscalculation, at least as regarded Ptolemy and his

The vast temple at
Dendera (above), an
ancient site of Upper
Egypt, was originally
consecrated to the
mother goddess Hathor.
The Ptolemies built an
adjacent temple to Isis,
merging the two deities.
To retain the support of
the powerful Egyptian
priesthood and the mass
of the faithful, Cleopatra
went to Erment, near
Thebes, to celebrate the
ritual enthronement of
the bull Buchis, an incar-
nation of the ancient
god Montu, protector
of the pharaoh. Left:
a stele commemorates
the ceremony.

advisors. Photinus and Theodotus, after weighing the advantages and disadvantages of taking Pompey in, decided that the Roman must die; they would thus earn Caesar's gratitude, while Pompey could not take revenge. Plutarch reported Theodotus's grim axiom: "Dead men don't bite."

Three days later, on 2 October, Caesar sailed within sight of Pelusium, escorted by two legions—120 men— and 800 cavalry. Still unaware of Pompey's fate, he stayed prudently aboard his ship, where Theodotus brought his tribute: the head of Pompey and his ring. Caesar wept, it is said, at the sight of these mournful tokens; then, reassured by the Egyptians' attitude, he officially entered Alexandria, preceded by his *lictors*. Cleopatra's destiny now depended on him.

The queen meets Caesar

Caesar entered the city as a conqueror. The discontented populace rose up, and many Roman soldiers were killed in skirmishes, until he soothed the crowd with his usual skill, reminding the Alexandrians that as consul he represented Roman law, and averring that he had urged the treaty recognizing Auletes' sovereignty. He summoned both Cleopatra and her brother in order to settle the conflict between them. Photinus immediately brought Ptolemy back to Alexandria, but kept the Egyptian army intact, leaving it at Pelusium, under the command of Achillas.

Cleopatra was more cautious, sending several emissaries to Caesar before trusting his good intentions. Finally, she agreed to come to Alexandria, but fearing her brother's spies and his attempts to impede her, she

In September 48 BCE, Caesar (right, in a marble portrait bust, 1st century CE), the new strongman of Rome, arrived at the gates of Alexandria, forcing Cleopatra to flee. Pompey (left, in a coin) had just been traitorously assassinated by order of Ptolemy XIII, the queen's brother-husband, whom he had believed would shelter him. Pompey had been Caesar's last rival in the East.

"Among his mistresses were several queens— including Eunoë, wife of Bogudes the Moor.... The most famous of these queens was Cleopatra of Egypt."
Suetonius, *The Twelve Caesars*, c. 121 CE

A fine writer, art lover, and brilliant military leader, the fifty-two-year-old Julius Caesar was equally famous for his love affairs. His secret meeting with the young queen was fateful: beyond their passion, their interests were entwined. This alliance with a powerful ruler whose riches were legend was to Caesar's advantage, yet Cleopatra needed his support even more to regain her throne. This unequal balance of power is shown reversed in a 19th-century painting by Jean-Léon Gérôme (right), in which the queen appears to dominate Caesar.

arrived secretly, in the dead of night, and hidden, Plutarch wrote, wrapped "in a coverlet," or, according to others, rolled in a carpet. And so it was that the astonished Caesar discovered the young queen of Egypt, smuggled into his apartments. That they became lovers is known, perhaps for reasons of political convenience; but the attraction between two powerful people of high lineage must have been strong.

Early the following morning, Caesar summoned Ptolemy, who, furious at seeing his sister at the Roman's side, cast his diadem to the floor and went raging out of the palace, shouting accusations of treason. A riot was narrowly averted: Caesar called the people and read them Auletes' will, representing himself as its executor. He declared his goodwill toward Egypt and his wish to reconcile its rulers, and even promised to give back the island of Cyprus, to be governed by

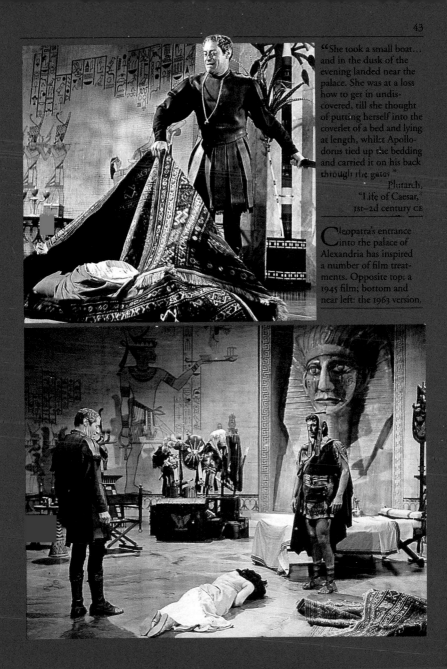

"She took a small boat… and in the dusk of the evening landed near the palace. She was at a loss how to get in undiscovered, till she thought of putting herself into the coverlet of a bed and lying at length, whilst Apollodorus tied up the bedding and carried it on his back through the gates."
Plutarch,
"Life of Caesar,"
1st–2d century CE

Cleopatra's entrance into the palace of Alexandria has inspired a number of film treatments. Opposite top: a 1945 film; bottom and near left: the 1963 version.

Cleopatra's siblings, Arsinoë and the
youngest Ptolemy. A great banquet celebrated
the accord between brother and sister.

The three then began an odd life together. Caesar
settled in Alexandria, giving himself over to courses in
philosophy, scientific conferences, tours of the city,
and Cleopatra's love. The young woman once more
sat on her throne in the imperial palace, beside her lover
and protector. Ptolemy XIII lived with them, more
hostage than king.

Alexandria in flames

The young pharaoh, however, continued to plot
with Arsinoë and Photinus, waging a secret war of

Ptolemy XIII was still a
prisoner in the palace;
Photinus had been
executed after attempting
to poison Caesar; but
Arsinoë managed to
escape. She reached the
Egyptian camp with her
foster-father, the eunuch
Ganymedes, who had his
ally Achillas put to death
and took command of
the army. The Egyptians
assembled a fleet, seized
the island of Pharos, and
surrounded the royal
palace. After a difficult
battle, Caesar retook
the island. But as his
men were building the
scaffolding for a causeway
to connect Pharos to the
mainland, a tremendous
brawl broke out, causing
the legionnaires to flee in
panic. Above: the event as
depicted the 1963 Joseph
Mankiewicz film.

intrigues against his sister and the Roman consul. With shameless lies, the conspirators stirred up the Alexandrians' animosity. Finally, at the end of October 48 BCE, at their command, Achillas, who had remained at Pelusium, marched on Alexandria at the head of twenty thousand Egyptian infantry and two thousand cavalry. Caesar and Cleopatra attempted to negotiate, but in vain. Civil war erupted.

While Cleopatra and Caesar occupied the royal palace, holding Ptolemy XIII, Achillas's army occupied the rest of the city, trying to take the Great Harbor, where seventy-two Egyptian warships and fifty Roman *triremes* were at anchor. In order to keep them out of the enemy's hands, Caesar had the vessels set on fire. The roaring flames leapt onto the quays, engulfing buildings and granaries, finally reaching the great library, which may have been at least partly burned. For weeks the battle stormed in the streets, with first one faction prevailing, then the other. Ptolemy was released from house arrest, and joined Achillas. After several months of combat, Caesar, aided by the arrival of reinforcements and Ptolemy's military incompetence, put the Egyptians to flight, pressing them toward the Nile, where they drowned by the hundreds. Among them was the young pharaoh, whose body, discovered in the mud, was identified by his golden breastplate.

Caesar brought Ptolemy's breastplate in triumph back to Alexandria, where the populace

During the battle Caesar's own boat sank under the onslaughts of the Egyptians; he cheated death by swimming in full armor to the nearest ship. Heartened by victories, the Alexandrians demanded Ptolemy, whom Caesar released willingly, convinced that this would serve him in the long run. His foresight was vindicated: Ptolemy was utterly incompetent militarily. The Alexandrians were promptly defeated at sea, and in March 47 BCE, Caesar marched on Ptolemy's camp at the head of an army that included troops sent by Mithradates of Pergamum. Rome won the day.

It is often said that the Library (possibly at left) was destroyed in the war, but this is not certain. Mark Antony partly rebuilt or renovated it, with 200,000 volumes brought from Pergamum, but the edifice had disappeared by the 4th century CE.

In this 17th-century painting, Pietro da Cortona portrayed Caesar (center) in traditional fashion, his head crowned with laurels, wearing the purple mantle of a general, and leading an almost submissive young Cleopatra to the throne, beneath the annoyed gaze of Arsinoë (right), thus definitively dispossessed from the power she had sought. At left are the two faithful servants Iras and Charmion, while the soldiers looming in the background most likely represent the legionnaires that Caesar left in Alexandria to protect the queen.

begged for mercy, dressed in mourning and prostrate before him. It was 27 March 47 BCE; Cleopatra's lover was Egypt's master.

Cleopatra's triumph

Cleopatra had regained her throne yet again, and was technically a widow at twenty-two. Following tradition, she now married her second brother, the youngest Ptolemy, who became Ptolemy XIV. But the new pharaoh was some ten years old, and Cleopatra and Caesar held the reins of

In the spring of 47 BCE, Caesar and Cleopatra sailed up the Nile with an escort of forty ships to show the country its victorious new ruler, supported by the might of Rome. Because the ancients gave so little information on this episode, the imagination of generations of artists has run wild. Below: the painter H. Pilou envisions a Beaux-Arts extravaganza.

power. Arsinoë was imprisoned and sent to Rome. In Alexandria Caesar established a Roman guard of three legions whose duty was to protect the queen. He took measures to pacify the capital, and granted the freedom of the city to the Alexandrian Jews, who had supported him during the troubles. In the spring of 47 BCE, the Imperator accompanied Cleopatra on a long voyage up the Nile aboard a luxurious pleasure barge. Depicted as a lovers' outing, it was a political tour intended to show the people of the country their masters.

"Despite my strong interest in science," said Caesar to Acoreus, the priest of Isis, "nothing would satisfy my intellectual curiosity more fully than to be told what makes the Nile rise. If you can enable me to visit its source, which has been a mystery for so many ages, I promise to abandon this civil war."
Lucan,
Civil War, Book X,
c. 62 CE

For Caesar, this was a research trip as well: hoping to succeed where Alexander the Great had failed, he was searching for the mysterious sources of the Nile—which were not in fact discovered until the 19th century.
Lucan related that he spent half a night discussing the subject with the Alexandrian scholar Acoreus.

Cleopatra was pregnant when Caesar left Egypt in May for his lightninglike eastern campaign, the occasion for his famous summary *"veni, vidi, vinci"*—"I came, I saw, I conquered."

A son for Caesar?

On 23 June 47 BCE Cleopatra gave birth to her first child, a boy, who was given the name Ptolemy Caesar, but whom the people of Alexandria instantly named Caesarion. (The well-informed Caesar seems to have allowed the name to stick.) Cleopatra ordered coins to be struck on which she appeared as Isis-Aphrodite, holding Horus-Eros in her arms. She had the walls of the temple at Erment, near Thebes, decorated with a scene celebrating the child's birth. Cleopatra was depicted at the god Amon's side, while the gods presided over the arrival of the divine child. The priests zealously proclaimed that young Caesarion had been fathered by the god Amon-Ra, in the human shape of Caesar. The child was thus legitimate, and the Egyptian traditions respected.

The queen at the foot of the Capitol

It was probably in the summer of 46 BCE that Cleopatra

left Egypt—where her power was now well assured—for Rome and Caesar. With her she took her son and her figurehead husband. She may have attended the fourfold Triumph that the Imperator—by now virtually ruler of the empire—organized that year to celebrate his victories over Gaul, Egypt, Pontus, and Africa. The spectators watched the triumphal procession to the Capitoline hill go by, with its prisoners and masses of treasure, its effigies of the dead traitors Photinus and Achillas, statues of the personified Nile and the Lighthouse, and, in person, the young Arsinoë in chains. At nightfall, Caesar came down from the Capitol, preceded by forty elephants bearing flaming cressets. As was the custom, the soldiers heckled their general, joking about his amatory as well as military successes. Caesar took it all in good part, well knowing that what the soldiers called out aloud and smiling, many citizens resentfully kept to themselves.

Indeed, in Rome the grumbling against "the Egyptian woman" was increasing—to the Romans, she symbolized both the dangers of a monarchy and the threat of soft, foreign, Oriental ways. After all, Caesar was married to a respectable Roman matron, Calpurnia, whom he had wed in 49 BCE. Cicero's was the most eloquent voice of this hostility: amid a crowd of sycophants, the orator came to pay the queen his compliments, with the excuse of borrowing a scholarly work, but never forgave her the casualness with which

"[Caesar] even allowed her to call the son whom she had borne him by his own name. Some Greek historians say that the boy closely resembled Caesar in features as well as in gait."

Suetonius,
The Twelve Caesars,
c. 121 CE

Was the child born shortly after Caesar left Egypt his or not? The question has remained unanswered. Some—mainly Romans—maintained that the child was only a bastard son of the queen's. Cleopatra named him Ptolemy Caesar and had herself represented with him on bas-reliefs in temples at Dendera and Erment; she was anxious to legitimate him in the eyes of the Egyptian priesthood, and identified herself with Isis and her son with Horus, son of the goddess. At Erment a bas-relief of the *mammisi,* or birth temple (far left, in a drawing after the original) portrays the birth of Horus, called Harpocrates, protected by the sacred scarab and surrounded by a multitude of gods, among whom she takes her place. In a relief at Dendera (near left), Caesarion presents an offering to Isis-Cleopatra. Late Ptolemaic statues of Isis holding the child Horus further sustained the identification with the Cleopatra-Caesarion pair.

she received him. From then on, he attacked her incessantly in his private correspondence, declaring that "all evil comes from Alexandria." Yet Caesar had

taken care to settle Cleopatra outside the city proper, across the Tiber in the sumptuous gardens where he had a villa.

Caesar conquered public opinion as well: he rendered official homage to the queen by having a golden statue of Cleopatra-Venus placed in the Temple of Venus Genitrix in the Forum Julium, which he had just built. Not only was Venus the tutelary goddess of the Roman people, but Caesar also claimed for his family, the Iulii, an illustrious descent from the goddess herself. He was thus associating an apotheosized Oriental ruler with an ancestral national goddess, and perhaps implying divine ancestry for the child Caesarion.

Alone again: the Ides of March, 44 BCE

Caesar's power continued to increase: in 46 BCE he became dictator for ten years, consul for ten years, and prefect of public morals for three years. In February 44 BCE the Senate named him dictator for life. There was a rumor that he wanted to overthrow the Senate and become absolute king, but when during the ceremonies

Julius Caesar was assassinated during a session of the Senate in 44 BCE by republican conspirators who feared his power. Above: an 1889 fresco of the ancient Roman Senate. "Some say...that when he saw Brutus's sword drawn, he covered his face with his robe and submitted.... [He] breathed out his soul through his multitude of wounds, for they say he received three-and-twenty."
Plutarch,
"Life of Caesar,"
1st–2d century CE

for the Lupercalia festival of 14 February 44 BCE Mark Antony offered him a crown, he ostentatiously refused it three times. His refusals failed to assuage the fears of his enemies or deter their planned assassination. One month later, on 15 March 44 BCE, the Ides (as the middle of the month was called), during a session of the Senate, conspirators—including Brutus, almost certainly his natural son—struck Caesar down at the foot of the statue of Pompey. Cleopatra had lost her powerful ally, and had to flee the Italian capital, boarding a ship for Alexandria with her husband and child. This gave Cicero cause for rejoicing: "The Queen's flight does not distress me," he wrote his friend Atticus on 16 April of that year.

"I hate the Queen.… The Queen's insolence, too, when she was living in Caesar's house in the gardens beyond the Tiber, I cannot recall without indignation."
Cicero, Letter to Atticus, 13 June 44 BCE

Cicero (above, in a 1st-century BCE marble bust) was a fervent supporter of the Republic who detested Cleopatra and the Oriental monarchies as much as he hated Caesar. He did not, however, take part in the conspiracy.

Left: The assassination of Julius Caesar in a 1797 painting.

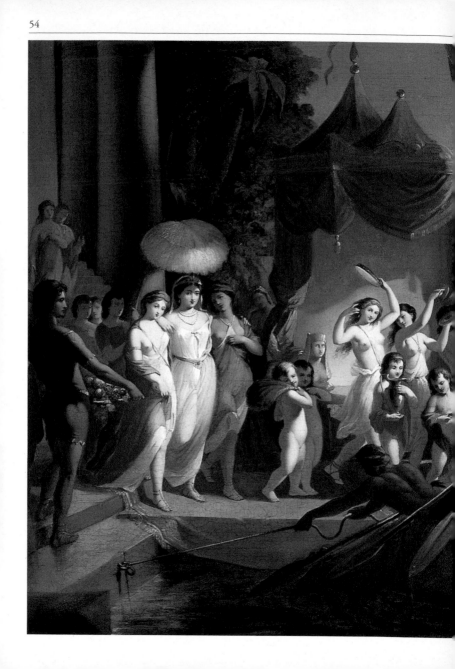

Problems awaited Cleopatra upon her return from Rome: a usurper acting on Arsinoë's orders had passed himself off as Ptolemy XIII, sowing confusion; in 42 and 41 BCE the Nile did not rise high enough to refertilize the land, causing famine and plague. But it was the international situation that most preoccupied the queen: in Rome, Mark Antony and Octavian were competing to succeed Caesar. What policy would the winner pursue toward Egypt?

CHAPTER 3
SOVEREIGN IN THE EAST

"I shall not be the first woman to rule the Nile valley; we have no law against female...sovereignty."

Lucan,
Civil War, Book X,
c. 62 CE

Left: a painting of Cleopatra leaving Rome; right: her cartouche, with her name in hieroglyphics.

At the death of Ptolemy XIV, little Ptolemy Caesar became pharaoh at his mother's side. Once again, Cleopatra was the country's sole ruler.

Rome torn asunder: the prudence of Cleopatra

Julius Caesar's death threw Italy into crisis. Two ambitious men competed to succeed him in control of the Imperium: Mark Antony, the designated consul, and the young Octavian, named by Caesar as his adopted son and legal heir. Civil war broke out, and Mark Antony was defeated in a battle at Modena on 21 April 43 BCE. But opposition to Octavian was brewing among the defenders of the Republic responsible for Caesar's death, who had fled with an army of supporters to the East. Brutus in Macedonia and Cassius in Syria fought the Caesarian general Dolabella. This Italian war moved closer to Egypt, and Cleopatra, acting with great prudence, refused to support either side. She had every reason to fear the

The hot-headed consul Mark Antony (left, in a Roman marble portrait) had been a friend of Julius Caesar; supported by his troops and generally very popular, he appeared to be the new master of Rome. Octavian (right, in a Roman bronze portrait), Caesar's grand-nephew and legal heir, enjoyed the support of Cicero and many of the senators. Suetonius said of him: "Augustus' eyes were clear and bright, and he liked to believe that they shone with a sort of divine radiance."

Suetonius,
The Twelve Caesars,
C. 121 CE

republicans, even though the Roman legions stationed in Alexandria joined Cassius; and despite public statements implying that she would give aid to the Caesarians, she in fact sent Dolabella neither ships, nor men, nor provisions.

In Italy, though Octavian was gaining power, Lepidus, Caesar's former master of the horse, went over to Antony's camp, bringing with him the western provinces. Rather than see all power slip his grasp entirely, Octavian came to terms with his rivals. On 23 November, the Lex Titia officially sealed their pact for five years, creating the second Triumvirate—Antony, Octavian, and Lepidus. At the end of the year, the alliance was sealed in blood: the Triumvirs, aiming to eliminate all opposition, massacred hundreds of knights and senators. Among these was Cicero, who had written fourteen vehement *Philippics,* or attacks, against Antony; the latter

Older by some twenty years, and with a long military and political career behind him, Antony could not have been more different from Octavian, who was sickly, calculating, cold, and "very much a boy," as Cicero put it. Antony's was a passionate and generous nature; he was pleasure-loving and a trouble-maker, surrounding himself casually with fellow-revelers of easy morals. His soldiers loved him for his frankness and loyalty. He was extremely energetic when a situation required swift decision and action, but often nonchalant and lethargic otherwise; this instability may explain his penchant for strong-willed women. A lover of all things Greek, like many Romans, he was as skilled at sports as at "Asiatic" eloquence, whose ornate phrases and emphases stirred the enthusiasm of the masses.

The hideous bloodshed ordered by Antony and Octavian long symbolized the horror of civil war. Left: a 16th-century depiction of the slaughter.

had the orator's head and right hand cut off and exhibited at the Rostra, the speakers' platform in the Forum. There, it was said, Fulvia, Antony's wife, pierced Cicero's tongue with a hairpin.

Antony's triumphal tour of the East

The army of the Triumvirs, led by Antony, decisively defeated the republicans at Philippi, in Greece, in October 42 BCE. Cassius and Brutus committed suicide, while all the prisoners of rank were executed in a slaughter that the poet Lucan was to call "the funeral pyre of the Roman people."

Antony then began a grand tour of the East, partly in order to impose the Triumvirate upon the part of the world that had welcomed the republicans, but principally to collect the money necessary to maintain the Roman troops. The task was well up to his ambition, providing him as it did with the means to consolidate his power vis-à-vis Octavian.

With genuine pleasure, Antony traveled the roads of Greece to Athens, where he had once studied rhetoric. He remained there a time, becoming an initiate of the Eleusian mysteries. He then journeyed on to Ionia, on the coast of present-day Turkey, where, in the allied city of Ephesus, he was acclaimed "the new Dionysus" and entertained by a retinue dressed as bacchantes, satyrs, and Pans, to the music of flutes and harps. All was pleasure…though he did not neglect to exact exorbitant tribute and taxes. Little by little, he approached Egypt and Cleopatra. He crossed Mysia, Bithynia, Phrygia, and Cappadocia; he settled unrest in Judaea, despite opposition from the people, by appointing his friend Herod the Edomite and Herod's brother Phasael tetrarchs, or rulers. Antony finally stopped in Cilicia (now southeastern Turkey.)

"She was to meet Antony in the time of life when women's beauty is most splendid, and their intellects are in full maturity."

Plutarch,
"Life of Antony,"
1st–2d century CE

The meeting of Antony and Cleopatra at Tarsus was a diplomatic encounter between two political powers. But the queen went to great lengths to seduce the Roman general who held Egypt's fate in his hands. Left: a 17th-century painter imagines the scene.

Antony claimed descent from Hercules (below, in an Alexandrian statue), a symbol of

strength, courage, and virtue. He also identified himself with Dionysus (left: Hellenistic reliefs of silenuses, maenads, and satyrs). These were the same gods and demigods that the Ptolemies called their ancestors.

The meeting in Tarsus of Cleopatra-Aphrodite and Antony-Dionysus

In 41 BCE Antony moored his fleet at the Cilician city of Tarsus, at the mouth of the Cydnus River, and called upon Cleopatra to come and account for the support given Cassius by the Roman legions of Alexandria. This was merely a pretext, however, for meeting the great queen, though chiefly Antony wanted to know if he could rely on military and financial assistance from her. Like Caesar before him, Antony was considering an expedition against Parthia (in modern Iran), whose conquering army had arrived as close as Judaea, and now threatened the Roman protectorates in the region. Antony dreamed of a

The romantic episode that Plutarch describes as the meeting of Antony and Cleopatra has provided painters with inexhaustible sources of inspiration. In the 1740s Giovanni Battista Tiepolo devoted two frescoes in Palazzo Labia in Venice to this theme. Left: Antony attentively receives Cleopatra as she alights from her gilded galley. Right: during the magnificent banquet that the queen has arranged for Antony, Cleopatra captivates him as she prepares to dissolve a pearl in vinegar. Pliny the Elder cited this detail, which has become legend, though Plutarch did not.

stunning victory against this traditional enemy of the Romans.

As for Cleopatra, it behooved her to negotiate an agreement with the man whose star was rising in the East. Nevertheless, she kept Antony waiting, and only after several emphatic letters on his part agreed to leave Egypt to meet him.

Rumor, carefully fostered, said that the goddess Aphrodite, risen from the sea, was sailing down the Cydnus to visit Dionysus. Cleopatra had devised a spectacular arrival, which Plutarch described in his "Life of Antony": those on land saw "a barge with gilded stern and outspread sails of purple, while oars of silver beat time to the music of flutes and fifes and harps. She herself lay all along under a canopy of cloth of gold, dressed as Venus in a picture, and beautiful young boys, like painted Cupids, stood on each side to fan her. Her maids were dressed like sea-nymphs and graces, some steering at the rudder, some working at the ropes. The perfumes diffused themselves from the vessel to the shore."

Cleopatra answered Antony's invitation to dine on board his ship with an invitation to her luxurious vessel, where she offered him a sumptuous banquet, illuminated by innumerable torches. The feasting continued for four days, each more dazzling than the last. The young queen was twenty-eight years old, "in the time of life when women's beauty is most splendid, and their intellects are in full maturity," as Plutarch commented. Antony was forty-two: hungry for pleasure, he was in his glory as a victorious general. They became lovers and reached a political understanding immediately as well: Cleopatra secured Arsinoë's death and that of the pseudo-Ptolemy XIII. Thus rid of her rivals, she returned to Egypt to await him.

The inimitable life

Antony arrived in Egypt planning to spend the winter of 41 BCE there. He remained a year, passing his time between gymnasium and lecture hall, and in visits to monuments and sanctuaries. His status was that of a

Above: Cleopatra in a painting by Alexandre Cabanel, 1887.

"[Antony allowed] himself to be carried away by her to Alexandria.... They had a sort of company,...calling it that of the Inimitables."

Plutarch, "Life of Antony," 1st–2nd century CE

private citizen, though he exchanged the Roman toga for Greek dress, the *chlamys*. His life with Cleopatra was a never-ending round of parties and pleasures. The queen never left his side: she accompanied him to contests of swordsmanship, went hunting with him, played dice with him, offered him sophisticated banquets on jewel-studded plates. With a group of companions they formed a kind of fellowship, an intellectual and social elite, devoted to what they called the "inimitable life"—*amimetobios*—pursuing an endless joy, freedom, and intoxication with living; theirs was a mystique fashioned into a way of life. Cleopatra wore its name

"She had at any moment some new delight or charm to meet his wishes; at every turn she was upon him, and let him escape her neither by day nor by night. She played at dice with him, drank with him, hunted with him; and when he exercised in arms, she was there to see."

Plutarch,
"Life of Antony,"
1st–2nd century CE

engraved on a ring: *méthé*
("intoxication"). At night they
wandered the streets, dressed as
humble Alexandrians, or, often,
joined a group of revelers.

But the queen never lost sight
of the main point, never ceased
to remind the Roman good-
humoredly that she saw more in
him than an entertaining
companion. One day,
Plutarch tells us, she had
a salted herring hooked
onto Antony's line as he
fished Lake Mareotis and,
laughing at the stunned
angler, said, "Leave…the
fishing-rod, general, to us poor
sovereigns of Pharos and
Canopus; your game is cities, provinces,
and kingdoms."

Antony left Cleopatra at the end
of winter 40 BCE, called away by the
alarming situation abroad: Parthian
armies were occupying southern
Asia Minor, Syria, and Judaea, and
increasingly becoming a threat to
Rome. Herod was forced to take refuge in
Rome. Six months after Antony left,
the queen gave birth to twins: Cleopatra
Selene ("Moon") and Alexander
Helios ("Sun").

Antony, Triumvir in the East

Antony did not stop in Syria, but steered a
course for Athens, where his wife, Fulvia, had
provoked an uprising against Octavian, which
had gone awry. The encounter between husband
and wife was stormy and Antony, in a fury,
sailed to Brundisium (modern Brindisi, in
southern Italy). He never saw his wife again,
for she died some months later. After thorny

In Rome, as in Egypt,
marriage was an
alliance between families.
Octavian arranged a
marriage between Antony
and his sister Octavia
(left, in a Roman 1st-
century BCE bust), a
woman of "beauty,
honor, and prudence"
(Plutarch, "Life of
Antony"). In 38 BCE,
Octavian "took Livia
Drusilla [below, in a
bronze portrait] away
from her husband,
Tiberius Nero, though
she was pregnant at the
time. Livia remained
the one woman whom
he truly loved."

Suetonius, *The Twelve
Caesars*, c. 121 CE

preliminaries, Antony achieved an agreement with Octavian and Lepidus in October 40 BCE: the East would be his, the West Octavian's, and Africa would go to Lepidus.

Cleopatra had reason to be pleased with this division of the world, yet she was anxious, for not only did Antony remain in Rome, he remarried there. To seal their agreement, Octavian had given Antony his sister Octavia in marriage and their first child, a girl, Antonia Major, was born in the summer of 39 BCE. Despite the warnings of an Egyptian astrologer, Antony confirmed his alliance with his brother-in-law by inaugurating the new cult of the Divine Julius (Octavian's deified adoptive father), with himself as *flamen,* or priest. Italy seemed to be at peace at last, for in the same year the Triumvirs reached an accord with their last great opponent, Pompey's son Sextus, who was occupying Sicily.

But Rome also reinforced its position at the Egyptian border: a few months earlier, the Senate had named Herod—Cleopatra's enemy, but Antony's longtime ally—king of Judaea, Edom, and Samaria. The queen of Egypt had reason to be concerned.

A fragile accord

In the fall of 39 BCE, Antony and Octavian sailed to Athens, where they remained until the spring of 37. There, too, Antony lived the sybaritic life he loved: he was the patron of the gymnastic games; as the New Dionysus, he was joined in a mystical ceremony with the goddess of the city, Athena Polias, in the winter of 39. He gave the Athenians festivals and banquets—

Octavian's fragile health caused him to avoid physical exercise, whereas Antony exercised regularly and was a very good athlete. He also enjoyed organizing gymnastic contests, over which he presided as judge and which he financed in his capacity of *gymnasiarch,* or sponsor of the games. Left: a 1st-century BCE sculpture of an athlete.

usually paid from the tribute he extorted from them.

Meanwhile, his army had won two battles against the Parthians: his leadership in the East was beginning auspiciously indeed, but his relations with Octavian, who married Livia in 38 BCE, were once more becoming

Antony and Cleopatra had coins struck with their likenesses— an excellent medium for both domestic and foreign propaganda for the couple. On this silver coin the queen is on the reverse, the Roman on the obverse. Their profiles are treated in curiously similar fashion.

tense. War between them was narrowly averted, thanks to Octavia's pacifying intervention. In the summer of 37 BCE, Antony, Octavian, and Lepidus met in Tarentum, in southern Italy, and renewed the Triumvirate for five more years.

"His passion for Cleopatra broke out into a flame"

That fall Antony abruptly left Italy and Octavia, who was expecting their second child, and went east to the Syrian city of Antioch. Was love drawing him to Cleopatra, or did he need to renew his alliance with the queen, in view of the massive expedition he was planning against the Parthians? Cleopatra and the twins, his children, met Antony in Antioch, and there she married him according to the Egyptian rite, which unlike Roman law permitted polygamy.

Egypt's queen decreed that the years of her reign be renumbered from that moment. She led a life of luxury with

Antony in the Daphne quarter of the city famous for its laurel trees and cypresses, but did not neglect her ambitions. In exchange for financial support of his war she asked him to give her the territories of Coele-Syria and Judaea, which bordered Egypt. He granted her less than she asked for: the kingdom of Chalcis, the Syrian coast, Cyprus, and a few scattered areas in Cilicia, Crete, and Judaea, where King Herod functioned as a tax collector in the city of Jericho. Antony meant to keep this vassal and ally of Rome close to Egypt, despite—or perhaps because of—Cleopatra's enmity toward him.

A disastrous war against the Parthians

In the spring of 36 BCE, Antony, well-supplied with Cleopatra's money and troops, moved to engage the Parthians. The queen, pregnant again, accompanied him as far as the Euphrates River, then, in royal panoply, returned to Egypt, passing through Damascus and her new territories in Judaea. (It is said that Herod attempted to assassinate her; failing, he escorted her to Pelusium, on the Egyptian

Left: Elizabeth Taylor and Richard Burton as the lovers in the 1963 film.

Their union was sealed with the birth of twins, Antony "giving them the names of Alexander and Cleopatra, and adding, as their surnames, the titles of Sun and Moon. [He] would say...that the way to carry noble blood through the world was by begetting in every place a new line and series of kings" (Plutarch, "Life of Antony"). Antony was to have a daughter by his first wife, two sons from Fulvia, and two daughters by Octavia. Below: the lovers in a 19th-century painting.

border.) From Jericho Cleopatra brought back cuttings of balsam trees (called balm of Gilead in the Bible), which she planted in Egypt.

In Alexandria once more, Cleopatra ordered coins struck commemorating her enlarged empire. She and Antony were portrayed as paired Hellenistic rulers, new figures of Dionysus and Aphrodite, Osiris and Isis. But the child she bore to him that year was clearly identified with his Egyptian heritage: Cleopatra named Antony's last child Ptolemy Philadelphus, making him a true member of her dynasty.

In the meantime, in Parthia Antony suffered defeat upon defeat. He was forced to a dangerous retreat in the heart of an icy winter, his army decimated by dysentery, hunger, and the onslaughts of the redoubtable Parthian archers. In all, Antony lost twenty thousand infantry and forty thousand cavalry. The pitiable march ended in Syria, where the conquered general awaited aid from Cleo-

A presence on the Egyptian border, Herod the Great had governed the kingdom of Judaea since 40 BCE. An enthusiastic builder and fervently Hellenistic, he owed his throne to Antony's petition in the Senate. Below: a model of Jerusalem, one of his Judaean fortresses.

---

patra; though his soldiers were in rags, their misfortunes had in no way diminished their affection for him. Plutarch reported: "The obedience and affectionate respect they bore their general and the unanimous feeling amongst small and great alike, officers and common soldiers, [was such that they preferred] his good opinion of them to their very lives and being. For this devotion,…there were many reasons, as the nobility of his family, his eloquence, his frank and open manners, his liberal and magnificent manners, his familiarity in talking with everybody, and, at this time particularly, his kindness in visiting and pitying the sick, joining in all their pains, and furnishing them with all things necessary, so that the sick and wounded were even more eager to serve than those that were whole and strong." The queen of Egypt arrived with provisions, clothing, and money, and took the survivors back to Alexandria.

Cleopatra was very hostile to the Judaean king. According to the historian Flavius Josephus she "was secretly contriving the ruin of Herod." Her efforts were in vain—Herod's alliance in a region of uncertain borders was worth a great deal to Rome, and to Antony, who needed local support for his campaign against the Parthians (above: a statuette representing a Parthian warrior). East of Syria and Judaea, the Parthians had become aggressive after the humiliating and bloody defeat they had inflicted in 53 BCE on the Roman general Crassus, who had entered their territory.

Cleopatra's international policy

During the winter of 35 BCE Cleopatra engaged in intense diplomatic activity with neighboring states. She began by forging an alliance with the king of Armenia, sealed by the betrothal of her son Alexander Helios to the king's daughter. In Judaea Herod's mother-in-law, Alexandra, had begun an insurrection against him; when it failed

Cleopatra offered her asylum. Finally, she negotiated a treaty with the king of Media against Parthia; war there was once more a possibility. Despite the Armenian king's refusal to aid them, Cleopatra and Antony went on a brief campaign and reconquered the lost parts of Syria.

Fresh anxieties

Cleopatra was apprehensive. Trouble was clouding the western horizon, as Octavian, burning with seemingly limitless ambition, took Sicily from Pompey's son Sextus and Africa from Lepidus. As sole master of the entire region, he posed a powerful danger to Antony. More alarming still, Octavia, sent by her brother, had just set sail with provisions and ships to reinforce her husband's army.

Cleopatra moved heaven and earth to keep Antony in Egypt, out of the distant campaign—and away from his Roman wife. She lamented, wept, refused to eat: "When he entered the room, she fixed her eyes upon him in a rapture, and when he left seemed to languish and half faint away" (Plutarch). Whether or not she was dramatizing, she succeeded, and Antony broke with Octavian. He sent word to Octavia that he would not meet her, and sent her back to Rome, while he returned to Alexandria with Cleopatra.

A Roman-style triumph?

The disastrous Parthian campaign was in some measure erased by a swift expedition against Artavasdes, king of Armenia, who had betrayed Antony more than once. In the spring of 34 BCE, Antony, now settled in Syria, reached a new agreement with Herod, despite Cleopatra's hostility. He then occupied Armenia, imprisoned Arta-vasdes, took his treasury, and declared the country a Roman province. When he returned to Syria, he formed an alliance with the Median king.

The pharaoh's palace in Alexandria was considerably embellished as well

A 19th-century French Orientalist painter portrayed (left) a thoughtful yet dreamy Cleopatra in her boudoir, wearing fancifully exotic "antique" Egyptian dress and hair style (though she is seated on rather Victorian-looking furniture). The stone head above, found at Alexandria, shows her with the complicated coiffure of Alexandrian women, in which thin plaits are crowned with a high chignon.

as enriched by the Armenian booty, and in the fall of 34 BCE the Egyptian capital witnessed a sumptuous ceremony in honor of Antony's victory. An immense procession crossed the city to the square in front of the Serapeion.

Cleopatra, dressed as Isis, sat on a golden throne. Before her was set the chariot in which stood the victorious Antony, dressed as Dionysus, preceded by the king of Armenia and his family, wearing chains of silver in recognition of their royal rank; the trophies and spoils of war came behind. The reference to Cleopatra and Antony as heirs of divine blood was clear. At the end of the day, a gigantic feast was provided to the soldiers and people of the city.

The "Donations of Alexandria"

A few days later, in the immense Gymnasium, a sort of stadium, the Alexandrians attended an extension of the ceremonial triumph. Antony and Cleopatra, seated on high thrones of gold on a silver dais, presided over the assembly. On thrones lower down were seated King

The Egyptian capital was accustomed to magnificent processions staged by the Ptolemaic rulers as political ploys. Military victories were perfect occasions for these lavish festivities. Cleopatra and Antony mounted one such Ptolemaia in 34 BCE: a marveling crowd witnessed a procession of celebrants carrying statues of gods and former kings over flower-strewn ground, to the sound of flutes and songs, amid clouds of sweet perfumes. Above: a painter in 1903 imagined an Alexandrian festival.

Ptolemy, called Caesarion, thirteen years old, and the couple's three children: the twins—almost seven years old—Cleopatra Selene and Alexander Helios, the latter dressed as a Median king in an embroidered gown and high tiara adorned with peacock feathers; and Ptolemy Philadelphus, two years old, garbed as a Macedonian king in purple *chlamys*, royal cap, and little boots.

Antony gave a speech, reportedly in Greek, distributing the territories that were recent Egyptian acquisitions and those he had conquered. The pharaonic couple —Cleopatra, titled Queen of Queens, and Caesarion, King of Kings—received Egypt, Coele-Syria, and Cyprus. Alexander's share was Armenia and Media…and Parthia, yet to be conquered; Cleopatra Selene received Libya and Cyrenaica; and Ptolemy Philadelphus, northern Syria, Phoenicia, and Cilicia. All this, for the moment, was Cleopatra's to administer as regent.

It was the return of the great Egypt of the early Ptolemies— except that Cleopatra's realm was under Roman domination, clearly a vassal state. In Rome Octavian had a field day exploiting negative interpretations of the ceremony for propaganda purposes, claiming that Antony had placed a vast kingdom, as large as Italy, in the hands of his dangerous Oriental mistress.

Standing before the crowd, Antony gave Egypt and much of the Middle East to Cleopatra —the so-called Donations of Alexandria. Below: Elizabeth Taylor's Cleopatra, in a Hollywood-style procession.

74

Cleopatra was not yet thirty-five years old, and her power was in the ascendant. In Rome, Octavian could not tolerate this expansion of the Egyptian empire, supported by his former ally. Each side was preparing its weapons. The showdown was inevitable.

CHAPTER 4
A CLASH OF EMPIRES

"Cleopatra, the shame of Egypt, the lascivious fury who was to become the bane of Rome...the noise of her brazen rattle maddened the Capitol of Rome.... It seemed possible that the world would be ruled by a woman, and not a Roman woman, either. Her insolence began on the night when she first gave herself to Caesar... that abominable Ptolemaic princess."
Lucan,
Civil War, Book X,
c. 62 CE

Left: Cleopatra in a watercolor, c. 1887, by Gustave Moreau. Right: a portrait bust of Octavian.

While orators fulminated for and against Antony in the Senate, the political heart of Rome, Cleopatra continued her life with him in the East. Left and opposite: a scene in the Senate from the 1963 film *Cleopatra*.

Below: *Hercules and Omphale,* Pompeiian fresco, 1st century CE. "Antony, like Hercules in the picture where Omphale is seen removing his club and stripping his lion's skin, was over and over again disarmed by Cleopatra and beguiled away."

Plutarch, "The Comparison of Demetrius and Antony," 1st–2d century CE

While Cleopatra was consolidating her alliance with the king of the Medes, who would supply the Egyptian army with a cavalry corps, Antony and Octavian in Rome were fighting an increasingly bitter propaganda war that reached its peak in 32 BCE. Agrippa, Octavian's right-hand man, banished from the city anyone suspected of spying on behalf of the queen—including all the foreign seers and astrologers. Octavian himself had begun to establish a religious cult in his own honor: he built a temple to Apollo on his private land on the Palatine hill, in response to the mystique of Antony-Dionysus-Osiris that was developing at Alexandria. Supporters of both sides deployed lampoons and pasquinades; no attack was too low. Gossip circulated that Caesarion was not Caesar's son, that Antony

engaged in orgies
with Cleopatra, that
he had become an
Oriental monarch, under
the spell of a sorceress.
The two men engaged in an
acrimonious correspondence,
rife with accusations and
insults. Suetonius reported that
one day Antony curtly
answered
Octavian's
criticisms: "Do
you object to my
sleeping with Cleopatra? But we are
married; and it is not even as though this
were anything new—the affair started nine
years ago. And what about you? Are you
faithful to Livia Drusilla?" To the rumor that
he was always drunk, Antony replied with a
written speech, "On his intoxication," which
unfortunately has been lost.

The break

Antony wanted to avoid armed conflict, preferring to
remain within the laws and to have the Senate officially
recognize his authority in the East. To this end, he sent
his *acta*, or reports of his activities, to Rome at the end
of the year 33 BCE. Two of his supporters, Sosius and
Ahenobarbus, the consuls for 32 BCE, gave a passionate
reading of the *acta* in the Senate in February of that year.

Octavian—who had prudently surrounded himself with a group of friends and soldiers armed with daggers—responded with violence. A few days later, during another session, he denounced the "Donations of Alexandria." At that, the Antonian faction, faced with the increasing antagonism of the Romans, chose to leave Italy to join their leader in Ephesus. The rupture of the Triumvirate was complete.

Was Antony faithful to Rome—or were Octavian's attacks on his adversary and "the Egyptian woman" justified? The senators (left: a 1st-century BCE portrait of a consul) were undecided. In the East, Cleopatra and Antony stationed a huge army in their allied cities: Ephesus, Samos, and Athens.

Cleopatra, mistress in the East

Since the spring of 32 BCE, Cleopatra had been living with Antony in Ephesus, where they had gathered a vast army and fleet. Cleopatra appeared publicly as queen, escorted by Roman soldiers carrying shields bearing her cipher. With Antony at her side, she dispensed justice, presided over meetings, and reviewed the troops. She could be seen traveling across the city on horseback—or on a litter that, according to rumor, Antony sometimes followed on foot. Like all conquerors, she plundered the wealth of the region in order to send it to Alexandria, carrying off two hundred thousand *volumina* from Pergamum, and many statues and art

Right: an engraving of the Temple of Artemis at Ephesus; below: a reconstruction of Pergamum, which rivaled Alexandria in its splendor.

objects, most notably the Apollo of Ephesus and the Ajax of Rhoeton.

Cleopatra's prerogatives shocked even Antony's faction, who demanded that she be sent back to Egypt. Only the Roman Canidius defended her, understanding that the queen's presence was due as much to her wish to keep an eye on matters as to Antony's need for Egypt's riches and army in order to hold the East. Plutarch records that Canidius reminded Antony of the wisdom of a queen who had "long governed a great kingdom by herself alone."

In April, Antony and Cleopatra left Ephesus, now a strong military base, for the Aegean island of Samos, where they mixed business and pleasure, revels and strategic planning. In May they were in Athens, where the Athenians welcomed them effusively: statues of them as gods were placed on the Acropolis. In early summer Cleopatra achieved a great personal victory: Antony repudiated his

> "Antony…immediately sent Canidius with sixteen legions towards the sea; but he, in the company of Cleopatra, went to Ephesus, whither ships were coming in from all quarters to form the navy,…of which Cleopatra furnished two hundred, together with twenty thousand talents and provision for the whole army during the war…. When all their forces had met, they sailed together to Samos, and held high festivities. For as it was ordered that all kings, princes, and governors, all nations and cities [should bring] all munitions necessary for war, so was it also proclaimed that all stage-players should make their appearance at Samos."
>
> Plutarch,
> "Life of Antony,"
> 1st–2d century CE

wife Octavia, who was obliged to leave her home in Rome.

At that, close friends of Antony went over to the enemy's side, among them Plancus and Titius, who were privy to Antony's secrets. They told Octavian that Antony had made a will, now in the sacred hands of the Vestals. With careless sacrilege, Octavian seized Antony's testament and read it to the Senate: "Antony had borne witness to Caesarion," wrote Dio Cassius, "that he was truly sprung from Caesar, [and] had given some enormous presents to his children by the Egyptian queen, who were being reared by him, and had ordered that his body be buried in Alexandria by her side."

A declaration of war—Egyptian-style

The Roman people were furious at Antony's preference for non-Roman Egypt, their anger fueled principally by the last clause of Antony's will and exploited cannily by Octavian. Antony was stripped of all his authority, and Octavian made a spectacular declaration of war against Cleopatra: in front of the temple of Bellona, on the Campus Martius, dressed in the manner of the

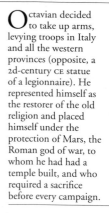

Octavian decided to take up arms, levying troops in Italy and all the western provinces (opposite, a 2d-century CE statue of a legionnaire). He represented himself as the restorer of the old religion and placed himself under the protection of Mars, the Roman god of war, to whom he had had a temple built, and who required a sacrifice before every campaign.

ancient Romans, he threw a wooden javelin, symbolically meant for the foreign enemy.

War was declared in October 32 BCE, not against Antony, but against the foreign woman, of whom Dio Cassius claimed that "whenever she used an oath, her strongest phrase in swearing was by her purpose to dispense justice on the Capitol." She was a dangerous

Above: soldiers register for the military and prepare a sacrifice to Mars, in a Roman stone frieze, c. 100 BCE.

enemy indeed who sought to enter the very heart of
sacred Rome!

A propaganda campaign against Cleopatra was
unleashed, while Octavian received oaths of support
from the states of Italy—Gaul, Africa, Sicily, and
Sardinia. Presenting himself as the champion of
freedom against monarchy, the West against the
Orient, Romanism against barbarism, Octavian set
sail eastward to confront Cleopatra and Antony,
then in Patras, on the west coast of Greece.

Actium: armies of Titans

Octavian led seventy thousand infantry and
twelve thousand cavalry; his fleet of four
hundred ships was commanded by the great
Agrippa. The army he faced, financed by
Cleopatra and commanded by Antony,
was far greater: besides the seventy-five
thousand legionnaires, there were
twenty-five thousand auxiliary
troops and twelve thousand cavalry;
of the five hundred warships,
two hundred were Egyptian;
three hundred cargo ships
accompanied them. Cleopatra,

aboard the *Antonia*, her purple-sailed flagship,
commanded her personal squadron of
sixty warships.

The two armies met on the west coast of
Epirus, farther north in Greece. Octavian
and Antony set up their camps on the
promontory of Actium, remaining there

face to face throughout the winter. The first skirmishes took place at sea the following spring: Agrippa captured all the neighboring islands. Antony's army, thus surrounded, was inadequately provisioned. His troops were thinning; the kings of Thrace and Paphlagonia rallied to Octavian. Worse, Dellius, one of his commanders, went over to the enemy, taking Antony's battle plan with him.

Cleopatra and Antony's only chance now was to try to run the Roman blockade with a skeleton fleet. Antony ordered the heavy cargo ships and the smaller, slower warships burned. The war chest was transferred to the queen's ship; "they first chose out the best of the vessels…; next they secretly put all their most valuable possessions on board by night," reported Dio Cassius. The ships' sails were not furled, as for combat, but kept ready to be hoisted for flight. Only four squadrons— 240 ships—remained, against Octavian's 400. All was ready for the escape by sea, while the army on land was entrusted to Canidius.

On 2 September 31 BCE, after four days of storm, a sea breeze rose around noon. The three squadrons of the fleet left their anchorage for the open sea, forming tight ranks in order to breach the barricade of Octavian's ships. Agrippa feinted and fell back. Gellius Publicola, Antony's co-commander of the right wing, launched his ships in pursuit, and Antony's front was broken.

With a sudden about-face, Agrippa attacked Antony's fleet, dispersing it. Cleopatra's squadron, which was bringing up the rear, took advantage of the opportunity to slip through a gap and make for the open sea. Antony leapt into a ship and followed, ordering his fleet to do the same. Some one hundred ships thus escaped Octavian.

Setback or victory?

Octavian's propaganda and tradition give an entirely one-sided version of this encounter: Octavian's victory was crushing and compre-hensive, decreed by the gods and nature itself. "True to her nature as a woman and an Egyptian [she] turned to flight," says Dio Cassius; Antony, blinded by passion,

This bronze *rostrum* is from a ship sunk at Actium. It was part of the prow, designed to stave in the hull of an enemy ship.

The stern of this ship (left) is adorned with a crocodile, the traditional symbol of Egypt. In this Roman sculptural relief the reptile, in chains beneath the sailors' feet, symbolizes a victory that Octavian presented as unambiguous.

The Romans were excellent soldiers on land, but less experienced at sea, and so attempted to transform naval battles into more familiar engagements. The *corvus*, or grappling hook, allowed them to link ships together, forming a kind of platform where they could fight hand to hand. Actium made Octavian more aware of the importance of maritime power; he reorganized the Roman navy, creating permanent fleets that protected private and commercial expeditions.

"abandoned all that were fighting and spending their lives for him…to follow her that had so well begun his ruin," says Plutarch. The defeat was total, says another chronicler, with the wreckage of the immense fleet floating on the sea, its luxurious purple and gold ornaments washing up on the shore.

Dio Cassius records that the war was presented to the Romans as a just war, not a civil war, since Antony was no longer Roman, as Octavian loudly maintained before the battle: "Therefore let no one count him a Roman, but rather an Egyptian, nor call him Antony, but rather Serapion; let no one think he was ever consul or Imperator, but only *gymnasiarch*." It was a glorious victory of the West over the East, of virtue over lax morals, of the Roman Republic over Oriental despotism.

Antony joined Cleopatra aboard her ship; they were free, and their treasury was safe. They may have been half-beaten, but they had eluded Octavian's trap.

"There is a harbour… where a bay lulls the roar of the Ionian Sea…. Hither came to battle the forces of the world…. On the one side stood a fleet doomed…and Roman javelins shamefully grasped in a woman's hand; on this, the flagship of Augustus [Octavian], its sails swelling with Jove's auspicious breeze, and standards now skilled to conquer for their fatherland…. The water quivered, reflecting the flashing of the weapons, when Apollo stood over Augustus' ship."

Sextus Propertius,
Elegies, Book IV,
c. 21–16 BCE

After Actium, Octavian was the sole, uncontested master of the Roman world. It was the unofficial end of the Republic; a new political regime now arose: the Principate, harbinger of the Empire. For Antony and Cleopatra, Actium meant the loss of a significant portion of their army and the defection of many allies. A year later, Alexandria was to fall, and with it, the Hellenistic kingdom of Egypt.

Left: *The Battle of Actium,* as reimagined in a 17th-century Italian painting.

The queen had no intention of returning to Egypt in the posture of defeat; instead, her garlanded ships sailed into the port of Alexandria to the sound of triumphal hymns. She immediately took up the reins of power again, executed a number of suspected traitors, and confiscated all their property. But she knew that she had not heard the last of Octavian.

CHAPTER 5
THE COMPANY OF DEATH

Plutarch writes that for three days Antony "sat alone, without a word, in the ship's prow, covering his face with his two hands," until they reached Cape Taenarum, in southern Greece. Only then did he come out of his silence and take up his life with Cleopatra again. They could not know it, but they were steering a course toward death. Left: the British painter Alma-Tadema interprets the theme of the lovers on shipboard, 1883. Right: an Alexandrian sculpture of a serpent.

A disheartening setback awaited Cleopatra and Antony at Cape Taenarum, at the southern tip of mainland Greece. The land forces they had left at the promontory of Actium had surrendered to Octavian for the price of an amnesty; the ships they had abandoned had almost all been burned. Aware of his weak position, Antony dismissed the handful of friends still faithful to him with generous gifts. He sailed to Libya to meet the four legions he had stationed in Cyrenaica, while Cleopatra went on to Egypt to await him. When Antony learned that these legions too had defected, his friends were hard-pressed to keep him from suicide.

Back in Alexandria, Antony sank into apathy. He had a small cell built for himself on the jetty by the port, and lived there as a hermit, retired from the court; he called it his Timoneion, referring to the legendary misanthropic hermit Timon of Athens. It took all Cleopatra's energy to bring him back to life. She organized feast upon feast: parties in honor of the coming of age of Antyllus, Antony and Fulvia's son, and of Caesarion's; and finally for her husband's fifty-third birthday. At length Antony consented to rejoin his friends, no longer practitioners of the "inimitable life," but now calling themselves a "company of death." They had agreed to die together, but meant to pass their last hours in mutual pleasure.

Escape—"a most bold and wonderful enterprise"

Cleopatra knew that Octavian would not stay in Italy, whither he had returned, but would soon address a situation that continued to irk him; he would seek to settle, once and for all, the conflict that pitted him against herself, and even more against Antony, to whom she was bound. She conceived a flight eastward,

R ight: a Roman cup with skeletons.

"They…broke up the Order of the Inimitables, and constituted another in its place, not inferior in splendour, luxury, and sumptuosity, calling it that of the Diers To-gether…, for the present passing their time in all manner of pleasures…. But Cleopatra was busied in making a collection of all varieties of poisonous drugs."
Plutarch,
"Life of Antony,"
1st–2d century CE

perhaps to India. She had the ships saved at Actium portaged to the Red Sea, so that she could take "her soldiers and her treasure to secure herself a home on the other side, where she might live in peace far away from war and slavery," as Plutarch wrote. But the Arabs at Petra (in modern Jordan), were allies of Octavian; they seized her ships and burned them. There was nothing left to do but wait for Octavian.

Antony fell into the deep despondency to which he was prone. Cleopatra continued to refuse to surrender him to Octavian. Below: a bust of an official, c. 80 BCE; opposite: a bust of Cleopatra.

Negotiate, Fight, or Die

In early 30 BCE Octavian reached Egypt's eastern border with an army; Roman legions under the commander Cornelius Gallus were stationed on the western border. The country was caught in a vise. Cleopatra and Antony attempted to negotiate, sending a trusted envoy to Octavian, charged with making the Roman an offer. Cleopatra wished to protect her children and ensure the continuance of the Ptolemaic line. Antony was prepared to renounce all his authority and return to private life in Egypt or Greece. "He offered to take his own life, if in that way Cleopatra might be saved," Dio Cassius says. Octavian did not answer Antony, but responded to the queen—who had sent him her scepter and diadem as tokens of her allegiance—demanding that she abdicate officially and have Antony executed. Cleopatra refused. The unhappy couple, plagued by doubts, went from suspicious quarrels to violent reconciliations.

According to Plutarch, by now "Cleopatra was busied in making a collection of all varieties of poisonous drugs" and, like her royal predecessors, prepared her tomb: a high, square tower, lit by two windows. There she piled up her immense treasure of gold and jewels, her furniture of precious woods, her perfumes, and a great deal of fuel to send it all up in flames, should her enemy try to take it.

When Cleopatra saw Antony die, her grief was overwhelming: her companion of eleven years was gone forever; she also knew that his loss heralded her own end and that of the dynasty of the Ptolemies.

In the spring of 30 BCE, Octavian's legions seized Pelusium; in early summer they were at the gates of Alexandria. Antony led a successful sortie with his cavalry, but the battle was not decisive; he then proposed meeting in single combat with his adversary, who refused contemptuously.

On 31 July Antony's army attacked Octavian. It was a diminished force, with only the infantry going into battle—his cavalry and navy had surrendered to the enemy. A rumor spread that the night before the battle the god Dionysus, Antony's protector, had left Alexandria in a great procession, to the sound of musical instruments. "The god whom Antony had always made it his study to copy and imitate, had now forsaken him," Plutarch observes. This was defeat indeed. The Roman legions remained at the gates of the city. Antony withdrew back to Alexandria.

A tragic misunderstanding

It was then that Antony heard a report from his generals that Cleopatra, entrenched in her mausoleum, had just died. He seized his sword, handed it to his slave Eros, and begged him to pierce his breast; but the young man used it on himself. Inspired by such courage, Antony stabbed himself in the belly—just as Diomedes, Cleopatra's secretary, burst in to announce that the queen still lived.

The dying Antony had himself carried to the mausoleum to see her one last time, only to find that Cleopatra had barricaded herself in to protect herself from Octavian's soldiers. With the help of two servants, she hauled her lover's bleeding body up through the window with ropes. "When she had got him up, she laid him on the bed, tearing all her clothes, which she spread upon him; and, beating her breast with her hands, lacerating herself, and disfiguring her own face with the blood from his wounds, she called him her lord, her husband, her emperor, and seemed to have pretty nearly forgotten her own evils." Thus Plutarch describes the famous scene. Antony urged Cleopatra to try anything to save her life "so far as might be honorably done," and then died in her arms.

Alessandro Turchi's 1635 painting *The Death of Antony* (opposite and below) recalls paintings of the Descent from the Cross: the bloodless body of the Roman evokes that

of Christ, and the queen's stricken posture that of Mary.

Octavian, master of Cleopatra

Octavian feared that Cleopatra, immured in her tower, would kill herself and set fire to her treasure. He wanted her alive and humbled, walking through Rome in chains in his triumphal procession, the object of taunts and jeers. He commanded Proculeius, one of his men, to do everything possible to take her prisoner. But Cleopatra would only negotiate through her closed door, and she sought only one thing: that her children should live and rule in Egypt. So Gallus, another messenger, distracted the queen while Proculeius entered the tomb by a window, surprised Cleopatra, and wrenched from her the dagger with which she meant to take her life. Thenceforth Cleopatra was a prisoner, closely guarded by Octavian, who took charge of her vast wealth.

...and of Alexandria

On 1 August 30 BCE, Octavian's army overran the city. To reassure the population, he gave a long speech in Greek, detailing his reasons for mercy: the beauty and wealth of the city; his admiration for Alexander, its founder; and his friendship with the Alexandrian philosopher Areios. Then he had the city searched for Antyllus, Antony and Fulvia's son, and for Caesarion. Antyllus was betrayed by his tutor, and his throat was cut where he had sought asylum, in the temple that Cleopatra had dedicated to Caesar's *manes,* or ancestral spirits. Caesarion was nowhere to be found—his mother had arranged his escape to India, by way of Ethiopia, with a large sum of money.

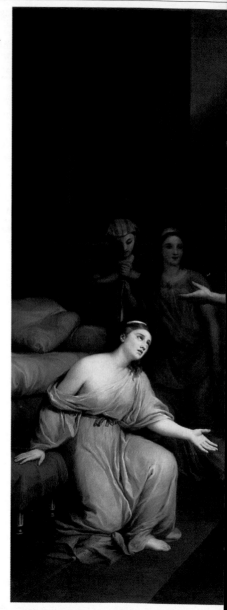

A queen's anguish

Octavian authorized Cleopatra to perform Antony's funeral rites, and she fulfilled this last task. She was determined to die rather than suffer the humiliation of Octavian's triumph. Unarmed and under constant surveillance, she stopped eating. The wounds she had inflicted on herself at Antony's deathbed were infected, and she was failing, undoubtedly with her doctor's complicity. Octavian threatened: if she continued on this course, he would cause her children to die "shamefully." At that, Cleopatra allowed herself to be treated and began to take food again.

Octavian finally came to see her. Dio Cassius, in his history of Rome, accused the queen of attempting to seduce her conqueror during this last meeting—"sweet were the glances she cast at him and the words she murmured to him." The businesslike Octavian would, of course, have resisted. Plutarch saw the scene somewhat differently: the queen—pale, wasted, her body feverish, her hair torn from her head in mourning—was in no condition to seduce anyone. She did, however, offer Octavian jewels, gifts for his wife and sister; she appealed to his pity. He believed she wanted to live.

> "He [Octavian] was afraid of losing a great treasure, and, besides, she would be no small addition to the glory of his triumph.... [He] himself came to make her a visit."
>
> Plutarch, "Life of Antony," 1st century CE

Did the queen in her mausoleum, during

their only meeting, beg the consul to let her live? Did she offer herself to her conqueror? Like some ancient authors, the 18th-century painter Anton Raphael Mengs suggests the possibility (left). No trace has ever been found of the mausoleum that, according to tradition, she built near the Temple of Isis (above, in an imaginative 17th-century representation).

A mysterious death

Cleopatra was to leave for Rome in three days. The moment had come. She visited Antony's tomb once more, then began her last preparations. Her two faithful servants, Iras and Charmion, bathed her, adorned her with cosmetics, and dressed her in a queen's robes; she ate a magnificently presented meal, then sent Octavian a tablet asking to be entombed beside Antony.

Too late, Octavian's people rushed to the queen: she lay lifeless in state, with Iras and Charmion dying by her side. Doctors and healers were summoned in haste, but nothing could bring the three women back to life. Had they used a pin dipped in poison hidden in a jewel? Had they set an asp to bite them? Someone remembered that a few hours earlier a peasant had brought her a basket of figs that might have concealed a serpent....

Cleopatra, thirty-nine years old, had chosen the only freedom left to her—death. She refused to follow in her sister's

Orientalist 19th-century painters such as Jean-André Rixens favored the mournful scene that the Romans found upon breaking into the mausoleum: Cleopatra and her faithful servant Iras lie dead, while Charmion adjusts the queen's diadem before also falling lifeless. Rixens has translated Plutarch's account: the queen lies nude, in an utterly abandoned posture that—painted in cool tones—is the undeniable sign of death.

degraded footsteps and allow herself to be carried in chains to Rome as a captive of Octavian's sword; her last ploy had been to lull her guard's watchfulness. Despite his anger, Octavian allowed her body to be placed beside Antony's in a tomb that has never been found. He ordered the statues made in Antony's honor toppled, but—for a large sum of money given him by Archibius, a friend of the queen—he agreed to leave her effigies intact.

Where Rixens painted conventional Victorian Orientalist decor —complete with panther skin—Valentine Prinsep (following pages) tried for historical accuracy. In his depiction of the same scene he included Greek and Egyptian elements that evoke the two cultures to which Cleopatra belonged. The warm tones and graceful attitudes of the figures suggest sleep rather than death. On pages 98–99: Frederick Arthur Bridgman produced an entirely fictive rendering of Cleopatra's funeral.

After the fall of Alexandria, Egypt came under Roman domination, but with a singular status: it was Octavian's personal property, and for four centuries was to remain a direct vassal of the emperor, while keeping its national character essentially intact.

CHAPTER 6

EGYPT—A ROMAN PROVINCE

After Cleopatra's death, Octavian became Egypt's new pharaoh, recognized by the priesthood as the living god. This hieratic statue (left), placed in the temple at Karnak, shows Octavian in the traditional attitude and with the traditional attributes of the Egyptian deity, but with his Roman curls showing beneath the royal headdress. Right: a coin in circulation after Actium: *Aegypto capta,* "Egypt has been taken."

A few days after Cleopatra's death, the Alexandrians were astonished to learn that their Ptolemaic king, known as Caesarion, pharaoh of Egypt, was returning to the capital, his tutor, Rhodon, having assured him that he had nothing to fear from Octavian. But Caesarion never reached Alexandria—he was assassinated en route, leaving Octavian as Julius Caesar's only surviving heir. Cleopatra and Antony's children were sent to Rome, where Octavia took them in. Alexander Helios and Ptolemy Philadelphus soon disappeared under suspicious circumstances; Cleopatra Selene alone survived.

Egyptian gold for Rome

Octavian seized Cleopatra's treasury and had her famous gold and silver plate and jewelry melted down. He plundered the royal palace, confiscated the property of Alexandrians suspected of aiding the queen, took two-thirds of the goods of the wealthy, and imposed burdensome taxes upon the city. Octavian's measures allowed him to pay his soldiers generously and to send to Rome a mass of precious metals so great that it caused the price of silver

These statues from the early years of Roman Egypt are eloquent amalgams of Egyptian deity and obviously Roman, human body. Left: The protective head of the hawk god, Horus, surmounts the body of a general, complete with breastplate. Right: atop a legionnaire armed with his lance is the head of Anubis the jackal, god of the dead, crowned with the disk of the sun. Such syncretism was a timeless Roman tradition: in order to appease both the people and the gods of a conquered state, the Romans took care to adapt their own deities to the latter, even building temples to the foreign divinities.

to drop by half, and the prevailing interest rate to fall by two-thirds.

The treasury of Egypt made up much of the sixteen thousand pounds of gold and the fifty million *sesterces'* worth of precious stones and pearls that Octavian shipped to the Temple of Jupiter Capitolinus, Rome's highest altar. He also chose works of art for the Italian capital. Myron's statue of Zeus, originally from Samos, went to the Capitol, together with a double portrait of Hermes, which was mistaken for a figure of Janus.

Octavian's triumph

Octavian traveled through Egypt as far south as Memphis, settling matters in the east and receiving the homage of Syria, Judaea, Phoenicia, and the Greeks in Asia. He returned to Rome in midsummer 29 BCE, during the month whose name he changed two years later, when he received the new title "Augustus," that is, "increased" by the approval of the gods. The Senate, the Vestals, and the Roman populace would have met him at his entry into the city, but Octavian refused the gesture as being too royalist—though within a few years he was to hold the reins of empire entirely in his hands. Many honors were conferred on him, including a three-day Triumph: on 13 August, he celebrated his victory over the Dalmatians; on the 14th, his victory over the Asians defeated at Actium; and on the Ides of August, the 15th, his victory over Egypt.

"Now all the processions proved notable, thanks to the spoils from Egypt,—in such quantities, indeed, had spoils been gathered there that they sufficed for all the processions,—but the Egyptian celebration surpassed them all in costliness and magnificence," Dio Cassius reports. The immense procession of men and riches that wended its way through the city toward the Capitol featured, besides allegories of the Nile and of Egypt, Cleopatra's twins, and a statue of their mother on her deathbed at the moment of her passing, a serpent coiled around her arm. "After this came Caesar, riding into the city behind them all. He did everything in the customary manner." For some time after, Cleopatra Selene embodied the memory of Egypt's last queen. Married to the learned ruler Juba of Numidia, who had been raised in Rome, she became queen of the province of Africa (Numidia and Mauretania), and founded, with her husband, a splendid capital, Caesarea —today's Cherchel, in Algeria—whose museum and library became widely famous. The coins struck with her likeness bore symbols of her Egyptian background: the sistrum of Isis, the cow Hathor, the ibis, and the crocodile. Following her death—and the

Given the Romans' hatred of royalty, after Actium Octavian (far left) had himself named *princeps*, or first among citizens, rather than emperor. This new regime—the principate—fed on an ideology of victory; Octavian's three Triumphs in Rome in 29 BCE went far toward his promotion. Left: a drawing reconstructing the Capitol, with the statues taken from Egypt standing before it.

Almost all statues of Cleopatra have disappeared; this head (below)—either the queen or her daughter, Cleopatra Selene—was found in Cherchel (formerly Caesarea), Algeria. The golden statue of Cleopatra placed by Julius Caesar in the Temple of Venus Genitrix remained there, it is said, for two hundred years before it too vanished.

assassination some time later of her son Ptolemy by the emperor Caligula—the Ptolemaic dynasty was no more.

Octavian, king of Upper and Lower Egypt, son of the Sun

"He did not see fit to inflict any irreparable injury upon a people so numerous, who might prove very useful to the Romans in many ways," observed Dio Cassius. Octavian had immediately become king of Egypt; now he intended to make the country accept him. There would be no reprisals against the people, he would show mercy toward the foreign prisoners, and though he kept the brothers of the king of Armenia as hostages, he sent Iotapa, daughter of the king of the Medes, back home.

As had his predecessors, he adapted himself to the pharaonic model and it was not long before he became an object of worship; he was the "beautiful child beloved for his amiability, king of Upper and Lower Egypt, son of the Sun, eternally living Caesar, beloved of Ptah and Isis." Statues of Octavian-Osiris, Octavian-Thoth, Octavian-Pharaoh began to appear everywhere; wearing the double crown of the pharaohs, holding the royal attributes, he too sat on the throne of Horus.

The cult of Octavian, initiated by the new government, was later spontaneously practiced locally.

After the end of the Ptolemaic dynasty, Rome left its mark on the Nile island of Philae, consecrated principally to Isis and Osiris. Augustus built a temple there, and colonnades, and had himself portrayed on the sanctuary walls. These were shrewd concessions to the local priests by a man who intended to reestablish the old Roman religion, and who expressed in Rome a fierce antagonism to the cult of Isis—despite its many adepts since Sulla's time. In 1850, the writer Maxime Du Camp, who visited the island with his fellow writer Gustave Flaubert, described the sight: "Here, everything dates...from the Greek and Roman eras, except for one propylon.... The overall effect of the ruins is splendid; when the setting sun illuminates them, one could be witnessing the remnants of a fairy isle. A portico supported by ten gigantic columns comes after [the] pylons; their shafts were once painted, the capitals still are. Beautiful tints of blue and white... vigorously accentuate the palm leaves and lotus flowers; it is magnificent." Left: the portico of the Great Temple, in a 19th-century engraving.

The Egyptian priests supported and legitimated the authority of Octavian, "the true heir to the gods' master," guarantor of order and prosperity in the country. Temples such as that built at Philae in 13 BCE were dedicated to the new pharaoh (temples were later erected to other Roman rulers in Egypt: Nero, Vespasian, Hadrian, and Caracalla).

Octavian was the first of a long line of Roman emperors—until the fourth century—to be divine pharaohs of Egypt; imperial visits such as Hadrian's in

"About this time he had the sarcophagus containing Alexander the Great's mummy removed from its shrine and, after a long look at its features, showed his veneration by crowning the head with a golden diadem and strewing flowers on the trunk. When asked, 'Would you now like to visit the Mausoleum of the Ptolemies,' he replied: 'I came to see a King, not a row of corpses.'"

Suetonius,
The Twelve Caesars,
C. 121 CE

130 periodically reignited the fervor of the faithful. This was thus the beginning of an imperial cult that soon pervaded the empire.

The new pharaoh, however, was more concerned with exploiting the country's resources and securing its possession than with respecting local traditions and the desires of the indigenous peoples; he meant to impose himself as Roman and conqueror. At the site of his victory, close by Alexandria itself, he founded a city, Nicopolis—"city of victory"; he recognized the Hellenistic god Serapis, but, unlike every new pharaoh before him, refused to bow before the divine bull, Apis, "declaring that he was accustomed to worship gods, not cattle," as Dio Cassius succinctly wrote. Back in Rome, he forbade, in 28 BCE, the building of private chapels to Egyptian deities within the *pomerium*, the sacred central precinct of the city, in which both dwellings and farming were prohibited.

And though in Alexandria he visited Alexander's tomb, he did not visit those of the

After Julius Caesar, Octavian most revered Alexander, the great conqueror and founder of Alexandria. He presented himself to the Alexandrians, indeed to all Egyptians, as the Macedonian's direct heir, although he conspicuously refused to identify himself with the line of the Ptolemies. The 17th-century artist Sébastien Bourdon placed Octavian— recognizable by his general's red cloak—at the center of his painting. He leads a procession of Alexandrians and points to Alexander's tomb, at left. The statue of Alexander's legendary horse, Bucephalus, rears up beside the pyramid.

ancient Ptolemies, distaining their lesser stature.

A province apart

Because of Egypt's strategic and economic importance, Octavian set up a unique system of management for it that distinguished it from the other provinces and that remained in place for four centuries. The country was absorbed into the emperor's personal domain. Its government was entrusted to a prefect of the rank of knight; the first of these was the poet and soldier Cornelius Gallus, a friend of Virgil, who was chosen precisely because of his modest social status (three years later, caught in a power play, he was disgraced and committed suicide).

Octavian altered the shape of Egypt in other ways. He kept the existing administrative structure, known for its great efficiency, but expanded it, adding the priesthood to the host of bureaucrats paid by the central government. Although the priests' land was taken from them, thenceforth they received salaries and were showered with honors, for the new pharaoh could not afford to alienate the all-powerful priestly class.

Because of the wealth and independence of Egypt, Octavian feared and meticulously regulated contacts between Rome and the new colony, which he surrounded with a version of a *cordon sanitaire*. No unauthorized senator could set foot on Egyptian soil, and no Egyptian who was not Alexandrian could become a Roman citizen. Octavian's attitude toward Alexandria itself was ambivalent: although he had to give consideration to the city's Greek and Jewish populations, upon whom he depended for support, he mistrusted them, and no Alexandrian was permitted to serve in the Roman Senate. Unlike the Greek cities, Alexandria had neither magistrates nor elected assemblies.

The Greeks and the Hellenized population of the city were the wedge that allowed Octavian to impose Roman domination on the land; he granted them privileges and exemptions from certain taxes, at the expense of the

Octavian founded the cult of the emperor that culminated in his own apotheosis (above, in a mid-1st-century CE marble frieze) after his death in 14 CE. The prestigious title "Augustus," granted him by the Senate in 27 BCE, already suggested a divine authority. Though he scrupulously refused any cult of his person, he permitted his divine *genius* or *numen* to bc worshiped.

"Lightning melted the initial letter of his name on the inscription below one of his statues. This was interpreted to mean that he would live only another hundred days, since the remainder of the word, namely AESAR, is the Etruscan for 'god' —C being the Roman numeral 100."

Suetonius, *The Twelve Caesars*, c. 121 CE

exploited and despised indigenous peoples. The official language remained Greek. The financial structure, with its complex system of mandatory record-keeping and taxation, became more elaborate and burdensome, especially for the peasants, who had to pay a head tax, the *laographia*.

The system of irrigation canals was expanded, and agriculture developed. The monopolies were eased, to the benefit of the Hellenized middle classes. Foreign trade increased. Egypt's wealth persisted until the 3d century, with the country becoming one of Rome's most productive granaries. Egyptian wheat, glass manufacture, and gold jewelry, papyri, wool and linen cloth, and perfumes continued to flow into Rome's port of Ostia and the other Italian cities.

Despite sporadic revolts, such as those of Hieropolis and Thebais, swiftly suppressed by Gallus, Octavian's initiatives molded the country's future for several centuries, until the reorganization of 395, when Egypt was folded into the (by then Christian) Eastern Roman Empire, and divided into provinces. For the moment, however, Octavian was its master.

Like Octavian, the Roman emperors who succeeded him were also portrayed as pharaohs. Unlike the Ptolemies, who adopted the traditional ancient Egyptian attributes and styles, the Romans imposed their own imprint. In this cult statue, below the pharaonic headdress, the face and hairstyle are typically Roman—a sign that the throne of Horus was now occupied by Rome.

Overleaf: a 19th-century evocation of the temple at Dendera.

DOCUMENTS

From history to myth

It is not easy to discern the historical truth about Cleopatra. Little archaeological evidence survives concerning her; her tomb has never been found and there are few extant portraits. Almost none of the ancient chroniclers were her contemporaries, and most of those who wrote of her were Greek or Roman, extremely suspicious of an Oriental monarchy—especially in the hands of a woman.

Cleopatra with asps in a 17th-century engraving.

Portraits of a queen

The Roman poet Horace (65–8 BCE) expresses mixed feelings toward "the Egyptian woman." A passage from his poem Nunc Est Bibendum *contains a grudgingly admiring portrait of a "barbarian" who displays the traditional Roman virtues of courage, pride, and stoicism.*

…A crazy queen was plotting,
with her polluted train

of evil debauchees, to demolish
the Capitol and topple the Empire—
…But the escape

from the flames of scarcely one ship
dampened her fury, and Caesar
dragged back to fearful reality
her mind swimming in Mareotic:

his galleys harried her fleeing from
Italy (just as the hawk the mild dove,
or the quick hunter the hare across
Thessaly's plains of snow), in order

to put the curs'd monster in chains.
  Yet she,
seeking to die more nobly, showed
no womanish fear of the sword nor
  retired
with her fleet to uncharted shores.

Her face serene, she courageously viewed
her fallen palace. With fortitude
she handled fierce snakes, her corporeal
frame drank in their venom:

resolved for death, she was brave indeed.
She was no docile woman but truly
  scorned
to be taken away in her enemy's ships,
deposed, to an overweening Triumph.
                                        Horace,
                        Ode, Book I, 37, 1st century BCE

Another Augustan writer, Sextus Propertius (c. 50–c. 15 BCE), refused even to name Cleopatra or Antony in this diatribe against Egypt.

What of her who of late has fastened disgrace upon our arms, and, a woman who fornicated even with her slaves, demanded as the price of her shameful union the walls of Rome and the senate made over to her dominion? Guilty Alexandria, land ever ready for treason. …To be sure, the harlot queen of licentious Canopus…dared to pit barking Anubis against our Jupiter and to force the Tiber to endure the threats of the Nile…. What profit now is it to have broken the axes of that Tarquin whose proud life gave him a title derived from it, had we been fated to bear a woman's yoke? Sing out your triumph, Rome, and, saved, pray long life for Augustus. Yet you fled to the wandering outlets of the Nile: your hands received Roman fetters….

Sextus Propertius,
Elegies, Book III, c. 24–22 BCE

In his epic poem, the Civil War, *also called* Pharsalia, *about the war between Julius Caesar and Pompey, the Roman Lucan (39–65 CE) wrote a vitriolic critique of Caesar, using Cleopatra's wealth and alleged immorality to attack him. Yet the queen's speech, as he records it, is a model of reasoning, regard for law and custom, and shrewd diplomacy.*

Cleopatra, the shame of Egypt, the lascivious fury who was to become the bane of Rome,…resembled Helen of Sparta, whose dangerous beauty ruined Mycenae and laid Troy in ashes; at all events the passions she aroused did no less damage to our country. You may

say, incredible though it sounds, that the noise of her brazen rattle maddened the Capitol of Rome; that she used the spells of cowardly Egypt to destroy Roman armies, that she nearly headed an Egyptian triumph and led Augustus Caesar a chained captive behind her. Until Actium had been fought it seemed possible that the world would be ruled by a woman, and not a Roman woman, either. Her insolence began on the night when she first gave herself to Caesar; it is easy to pardon Mark Antony's later infatuation when one remembers that she fired a heart so flinty as Caesar's. Despite his rage and madness, despite his bloody memories of Pharsalus, he consented in that palace haunted by Pompey's ghost to let an adulterous love affair complicate his military anxieties; and even begot a bastard son on the girl. What a disgrace to forget his daughter Julia, the dead man's wife, and posthumously present her with a half-brother, child of that abominable Ptolemaic princess! He even allowed his defeated enemies to rally in far-off Libya, while he wasted time on a sordid intrigue; and quietly deeded Egypt to Cleopatra instead of conquering it for himself.

She approached him in the manner of a suppliant, with a sorrowful face, but no resort to weeping, confident in her beauty. Though she had pretended to tear her hair in grief, it was not sufficiently disarranged to lose its attraction. "Great Caesar," she said, "birth may count for little, yet I am still the Princess Cleopatra, a lineal descendant of King Lagus of Egypt. I have been driven from the throne, and shall never regain it without your help; which is why I, a queen, herewith stoop to kiss your feet. Oh, please, become the bright star that blesses Egypt! If you grant my request, I shall not be the first woman to rule the Nile valley; we have no law against female sovereignty—as is proved by my father's testament, in which I am married to Ptolemy and appointed co-heir to the throne. Were Ptolemy only his own master, he would show that he loves me; but Pothinus dominates him. I am not pleading to inherit my father's monarchy; I simply want you to rescue our royal house from a shameful tutelage, and let Ptolemy be a real king by breaking Pothinus's ruthless hold on him. That presumptuous menial, who boasts of having beheaded Pompey, is now threatening your life as well—I pray the Gods that he will fail! It is pretty disgraceful for you, Caesar, and for all mankind too, when a fellow like Pothinus gains the credit of having killed Pompey the Great!"

Cleopatra would have stood no chance at all with stern-hearted Caesar, but for the evil beauty of her face and person; she bribed her judge and wickedly spent the whole night with him.…

Lucan,
Civil War, Book X, c. 62 CE

In his exhaustive compendium the Natural History, *the Roman naturalist Pliny the Elder (23–79 CE) wrote about the increasing ostentation practiced by his compatriots. Cleopatra figures in his tale of excess and splendor.*

Two only pearles there were together, the fairest and richest that ever have beene knowne in the world: and those possessed at one time by Cleopatra the last queen of Aegypt.… This princesse, when M. Antonius had strained him-selfe to doe her all the pleasure he possibly could, & had feasted her day by day most sumptuously, & spared for no cost: in the height of her pride and wanton braverie (as being a noble curtezan, and a queene withall) began to debase the expence and provision of Antonie, and made no reckoning of all his costly fare.… [She said] that she would spend upon him at one supper 100 hundred thousand Sestertii.… The servitors…set before her one only crewet of sharpe vinegar, the strength whereof is able to resolve pearles. Now she had at her eares hanging these two most precious pearles, the singular and only jewels of the world, and even Natures wonder. As Antonie looked wistly upon her, and expected what shee would doe, shee tooke one of them from her eare, steeped it in the vinegar, and so soon as it was liquefied, dranke it off.…

There was an end of one pearle: but the fame of the fellow thereof may goe with it: for after that this brave queen the winner of so great a wager, was taken prisoner and deprived of her roiall estate, that other pearle was cut in twaine, that in memoriall of that one halfe supper of theirs, it should remaine unto posterities, hanging at

An ancient coin with a portrait of Cleopatra.

both the eares of Venus at Rome, in the temple of Pantheon.

Pliny, *Natural History,*
Book IX, 1st century CE

A modern biographer, Lucy Hughes-Hallett, offers a syncretic analysis of a personality that continues to fascinate.

Cleopatra, whose banquet is as gorgeous an icon of plenty and of nurture as any cornucopia, resembles the mother who loves, as well as the mother who kills. Emile Mâle describes Terra, a pagan goddess who was still appearing in paintings in twelfth-century France. She is benevolent, generous, and "the serpent, son of the earth, drinks at her breast." Cleopatra, exposing her breasts in painting after painting, calls attention to her maternal bounty as, like Terra, she puts a snake to her nipple. As Queen of Egypt, the land which provided the Roman world with its wheat, she makes a fit avatar for the benign deity who presides over all growth, all fertility. Calmly handling her asps she resembles both her own chosen patroness Isis, and Isis's Roman counterpart Ceres, goddess of the earth and of generation, who appears in a Hellenic relief holding ears of corn, signifying abundance, and snakes, signifying life-in-death....

When Cleopatra/Venus disarms Antony/Mars she becomes a potently ambivalent figure, Venus Victrix, or Venus Armata, who carries her conquered lover's sword. Shakespeare's Cleopatra dresses Antony in her tires and mantles and takes for herself his "sword Philippan." Thus armed and virile she is an abhorrent and terrifying figure, the castrating *femme fatale* who usurps the male role. But she can also be taken for an image of wholeness. She is not only the female embodiment of love who has defeated the male principle of war; she is a double being endowed with the virtues of both male and female, commanding and dispensing both love and force. In her person goodness and greatness finally combine. Armed with Antony's sword, Cleopatra is a woman who has been spared the curse of womanly weakness. Holding the asp, the phallic beast which is one of her attributes and which does her will, she can lay claim to the wisdom of Tiresias, or of Athene who is accompanied always by a snake, or of Pythia, the oracular voice of Apollo, the priestess who knew all secrets, who was a female person, male god and snake in one....

Venus and Mars had a child, Harmony...Cleopatra, Queen of East and West, who contains both Venus and Mars, love and force, in her own person, who is both a mother and a phallic snake-woman, a woman and a man, is herself another Harmony, presiding genius of a Golden Age.

Lucy Hughes-Hallett,
Cleopatra: Histories, Dreams and Distortions, 1990

The men in her life

*To the ancients, Cleopatra was
an intriguing if incidental actor
in the larger-than-life drama of
Greece and Rome; she was seen
mainly as a political element in
the quarrel between the great
powers of the day. Today, popular culture has largely reversed
that view: the splendid Egyptian
queen tends to eclipse her
Roman counterparts.*

Julius Caesar

*The late-Greek biographer Plutarch
(c. 46–after 119 CE) describes a complex
public person—a writer, orator, leader,
and consummate politician.*

He was so much master of the goodwill and hearty service of his soldiers
that those who in other expeditions
were but ordinary men displayed a
courage past defeating or withstanding
when they went upon any danger where
Caesar's glory was concerned....

This love of honour and passion for
distinction were inspired into them and
cherished in them by Caesar himself,
who, by his unsparing distribution of
money and honours, showed them that
he did not heap up wealth from the
wars...but that all he received was but
a public fund laid by the reward and
encouragement of valour, and that he
looked upon all he gave to deserving
soldiers as so much increase to his own
riches. Added to this also, there was no
danger to which he did not willingly
expose himself.... His enduring so
much hardship, which he did to all
appearance beyond his natural strength,
very much astonished them. For he was
a spare man, had a soft and white skin,
was distempered in the head and
subject to an epilepsy.

Plutarch,
"Life of Caesar," 1st–2d century CE

Lucan's Caesar is less admirable.

In this royal banqueting hall Caesar
reclined, a power above all kings, and
Cleopatra beside him.... What madness
to parade this wealth before a guest
and thus excite his avarice, especially
when the guest was a Civil War general
greedily intent on enriching himself

with the spoils of all mankind.

The Roman biographer Gaius Suetonius Tranquillus (c. 69–after 122 CE) admires Caesar's good leadership—"in his administration of justice he was both conscientious and severe"—*and his civic and military ability. But the author of* The Twelve Caesars *is a confirmed gossip.*

Caesar is said to have been tall, fair, and well-built, with a rather broad face and keen, dark-brown eyes. His health was sound, apart from sudden comas and a tendency to nightmares which troubled him towards the end of his life; but he twice had epileptic fits on campaign. He was something of a dandy, always keeping his head carefully trimmed and shaved; and has been accused of having certain other hairy parts of his body depilated with tweezers. His baldness

The pharaoh Ptolemy Soter orders the building of the Museum.

was a disfigurement which his enemies harped upon, much to his exasperation; but he used to comb the thin strands of hair forward from his poll, and of all the honors voted him by the Senate and People, none pleased him so much as the privilege of wearing a laurel wreath on all occasions—he constantly took advantage of it....

The only specific charge of unnatural practices ever brought against him was that he had been King Nicomedes' bedfellow—always a dark stain on his reputation.... Bibulus, Caesar's colleague in the consulship, described him in an edict as "the Queen of Bithynia...who once wanted to sleep with a monarch, but now wants to be one."

On the other hand,

His affairs with women are commonly described as numerous and extravagant. ... Among his mistresses were several queens.... The most famous of these

queens was Cleopatra of Egypt....

A tribune of the people named Helvius Cinna informed a number of people that, following instructions, he had drawn up a bill for the commons to pass during Caesar's absence from Rome, legitimizing his marriage with any woman, or women, he pleased— "for the procreation of children." And to emphasize the bad name Caesar had won alike for unnatural and natural vice, I may here record that the Elder Curio referred to him in a speech as: "Every woman's man and every man's woman."

For the rest,

"He was not particularly honest in money matters [and] religious scruples never deterred him for a moment."

Suetonius,
The Twelve Caesars, c. 121 CE

Mark Antony

Plutarch disapproves of Mark Antony's lack of Roman discipline, which contrasts sharply with Caesar's austerity.

For some short time he took part with Clodius, the most insolent and outrageous demagogue of the time, in his course of violence and disorder; but getting weary, before long, of his madness, and apprehensive of the powerful party forming against him, he left Italy and travelled into Greece, where he spent his time in military exercises and in the study of eloquence. He took most to what was called the Asiatic taste in speaking, which was then at its height, and was, in many ways, suitable

Vivien Leigh and Claude Rains in the 1945 British film *Caesar and Cleopatra* by Gabriel Pascal.

to his ostentatious, vaunting temper, full of empty flourishes and unsteady efforts for glory....

He had...a very good and noble appearance; his beard was well grown, his forehead large, and his nose aquiline, giving him altogether a bold, masculine look that reminded people of the faces of Hercules in paintings and sculptures.... What might seem to some very insupportable, his vaunting, his raillery, his drinking in public, sitting down by the men as they were taking their food, and eating, as he stood, off the common soldiers' tables, made him the delight and pleasure of the army. In love affairs, also, he was very agreeable: he gained many friends by the assistance he gave them in theirs, and took other people's raillery upon his own with good-humour. And his generous ways, his open and lavish hand in gifts and favours to his friends and fellow-soldiers, did a great deal for him in his first advance to power, and after he had become great, long maintained his fortunes, when a thousand follies were hastening their overthrow.

This jovial good fellow was also coldly calculating and cruelly vindictive.

Three hundred persons were put to death by proscription. Antony gave orders to those that were to kill Cicero to cut off his head and right hand, with which he had written his invectives against him; and, when they were brought before him, he regarded them joyfully, actually bursting out more than once into laughter, and, when he had satiated himself with the sight of them, ordered them to be hung up above the speaker's place in the forum, thinking

thus to insult the dead, while in fact he only exposed his own wanton arrogance, and his unworthiness to hold the power that fortune had given him....

Plutarch, "Life of Antony,"
1st–2d century CE

Octavian, later Augustus Caesar

According to Suetonius,

Augustus was remarkably handsome and of very graceful gait even as an old man; but negligent of his personal appearance. He cared so little about his hair that, to save time, he would have two or three barbers working hurriedly on it together, and meanwhile read or write something.... He always wore so serene an expression, whether talking or in repose, that a Gallic chief once confessed to his compatriots: "When granted an audience with the Emperor during his passage across the Alps I would have carried out my plan of hurling him over a cliff had not the sight of that tranquil face softened my heart; so I desisted."

...His teeth were small, few, and decayed; his hair, yellowish and rather curly; his eyebrows met above the nose; he had ears of moderate size, a nose projecting a little at the top and then bending slightly inward, and a complexion intermediate between dark and fair....

Suetonius relates—and refutes—stories about assassinations engineered by Augustus, and balances tales of his remarkable clemency with episodes of deliberate cruelty.

As member of a triumvirate consisting of Antony, Lepidus, and himself, Augustus defeated Brutus and Cassius at Philippi.... After [a] second and decisive [battle] he showed no clemency to his beaten enemies, but sent Brutus' head to Rome for throwing at the feet of Caesar's divine image; and insulted the more distinguished of his prisoners. When one of these humbly asked for the right of decent burial, he got the cold answer: "That must be settled with the carrion-birds."

This same mix of ruthlessness and generosity characterized his behavior toward Antony and Cleopatra.

[He] took a roundabout route to Egypt by way of Asia Minor and Syria, besieged Alexandria, where Antony had fled with Cleopatra, and soon reduced it. At the last moment Antony sued for peace, but Augustus forced him to commit suicide—and inspected the corpse. He was so anxious to save Cleopatra as an ornament for his triumph that he actually summoned Psyllian snake-charmers to suck the poison from her self-inflicted wound, supposedly the bite of an asp.... He had the elder of Antony's sons by Fulvia dragged from the image of the God Julius, to which he had fled with vain pleas for mercy, and executed. Augustus also had Caesarion, Julius Caesar's bastard son by Cleopatra, overtaken, and killed him when captured. However, he spared Cleopatra's children by Antony, brought them up no less tenderly than if they had been members of his own family, and gave them the education which their various positions deserved.

As usual, Suetonius hits his stride in reporting gossip.

As a young man Augustus was accused of various improprieties. For instance,

Antony and Cleopatra in a 19th-century engraving after a bas-relief.

Sextus Pompey jeered at his effeminacy; Mark Antony alleged that Julius Caesar made him submit to unnatural relations as the price of adoption,...and that he used to soften the hair on his legs by singeing them with red-hot walnut shells....

[He] took Livia Drusilla away from her husband, Tiberius Nero, though she was pregnant at the time. Livia remained the one woman whom he truly loved until his death....

Not even his friends could deny that he often committed adultery, though of course they said, in justification, that he did so for reasons of state, not simple passion—he wanted to discover what his enemies were at by getting intimate with their wives or daughters. Mark Antony accused him not only of indecent haste in marrying Livia, but of hauling an ex-consul's wife from her husband's dining-room into the bedroom—before his eyes, too! He brought the woman back, says Antony, blushing to the ears and with her hair in disorder.... A racy letter of Antony's survives, written before he and Augustus had quarreled privately or publically:

What has come over you? Do you object to my sleeping with Cleopatra?

But we are married; and it is not even as though this were anything new—the affair started nine years ago. And what about you? Are you faithful to Livia Drusilla? My congratulations if, when this letter arrives, you have not been in bed with Tertullia, or Terentilla, or Rufilla, or Salvia Titisenia—or all of them. Does it really matter so much where, or with whom, you perform the sexual act?

Suetonius soberly concludes his review of Augustus's sexual mores:

Augustus easily disproved the accusation (or slander, if you like) of prostituting his body to men, by the decent normality of his sex-life, then and later....

And finally,

On the day that he died, Augustus frequently inquired whether rumours of his illness were causing any popular disturbance. He called for a mirror, and had his hair combed and his lower jaw, which had fallen from weakness, propped up. Presently he summoned a group of friends and asked: "Have I played my part in the farce of life creditably enough?"

Suetonius,
The Twelve Caesars,
c. 121 CE

Elizabeth Taylor and Richard Burton in the 1963 film *Cleopatra.*

Eyewitnesses to History

If we have few impartial portraits of the personalities in this story, we do have some excellent descriptions of the historical places and events they controlled. Though virtually nothing remains of the wondrous Alexandria founded by Alexander the Great, Strabo allows us to imagine the city, while Virgil takes us to Actium.

The Greek geographer Strabo, who lived in Alexandria during Cleopatra's time (64 or 63 BCE–after 23 CE), has left us a detailed description of her capital city. Recent archaeological discoveries have confirmed the accuracy of his account.

The advantages of the city's site are various; for, first, the place is washed by two seas, on the north by the Aegyptian Sea, as it is called, and on the south by Lake Mareia, also called Mareotis. This is filled by many canals from the Nile, both from above and on the sides, and through these canals the imports are much larger than those from the sea, so that the harbour on the lake was in fact richer than that on the sea; and here the exports from Alexandria also are larger than the imports; and anyone might judge, if he were at either Alexandria or Dicaearchia and saw the merchant vessels both at their arrival and at their departure, how much heavier or lighter they sailed thither or therefrom. And in addition to the great value of the things brought down from both directions, both into the harbour on the sea and into that on the lake, the salubrity of the air is also worthy of remark. And this likewise results from the fact that the land is washed by water on both sides and because of the timeliness of the Nile's risings; for the other cities that are situated on lakes have heavy and stifling air in

An 18th-century illustration of the civil war between Julius Caesar and Pompey. Left: Caesar's camp; right, that of Pompey.

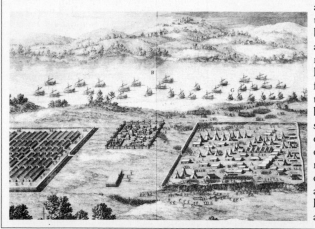

the heats of summer, because the lakes then become marshy along their edges because of the evaporation caused by the sun's rays, and, accordingly, when so much filth laden moisture rises, the air inhaled is noisome and starts pestilential diseases, whereas at Alexandria, at the beginning of summer, the Nile, being full, fills the lake also, and leaves no marshy matter to corrupt the rising vapours. At that time, also, the Etesian winds blow from the north and from a vast sea, so that the Alexandrians pass their time most pleasantly in summer.

The shape of the area of the city is like a *chlamys;* the long sides of it are those that are washed by the two waters, having a diameter of about thirty *stadia*, and the short sides are the isthmuses, each being seven or eight stadia wide and pinched in on one side by the sea and on the other by the lake. The city as a whole is intersected by streets practicable for horse-riding and chariot-driving, and by two that are very broad, extending to more than a *plethrum* in breadth, which cut one another into two sections and at right angles. And the city contains most beautiful public precincts and also the royal palaces, which constitute one-fourth or even one-third of the whole circuit of the city; for just as each of the kings, from love of splendour, was wont to add some adornment to the public monuments, so also he would invest himself at his own expense with a residence, in addition to those already built, so that now, to quote the words of the poet, "there is building upon building." All, however, are connected with one another and the harbour, even those that lie outside the harbour. The Museum is also a part of the royal palaces; it has a public walk, an Exedra

E lizabeth Taylor interprets the role of Cleopatra in 1963.

with seats, and a large house, in which is the common mess-hall of the men of learning who share the Museum. This group of men not only hold property in common, but also have a priest in charge of the Museum, who formerly was appointed by the kings, but is now appointed by Caesar. The Soma also, as it is called, is a part of the royal palaces. This was the enclosure which contained the burial-places of the kings and that of Alexander....

Strabo,
Geography, 1st century CE

*The Roman poet Virgil (70–19 BCE)
described the naval battle of Actium, of
which he no doubt received direct reports,
in a scene in his epic poem, the* Aeneid.
In the heroic mode of Homer, the poet

describes a conflict of divine proportions, but his message contains an updated nationalism: God is on Rome's side.

Ranged on the line opposed, Antonius brings
Barbarian aids and troops of Eastern kings,...
His ill fate follows him—the Egyptian wife.
Moving they fight: with oars and forky prows
The froth is gathered, and the water glows.
It seems as if the Cyclades again
Were rooted up and jostled in the main,
Or floating mountains floating mountains meet,
Such is the fierce encounter of the fleet.
Fireballs are thrown, and pointed javelins fly;

Two ships clash in battle in the 1963 film *Cleopatra.*

The fields of Neptune take a purple dye.
The queen herself, amidst the loud alarms,
With cymbals tossed her fainting soldiers warms—
Fool as she was, who had not yet divined
Her cruel fate, nor saw the snakes behind.
Her country gods, the monsters of the sky,
Great Neptune, Pallas, and love's queen defy.
The dog Anubis barks, but barks in vain,
No longer dares to oppose the ethereal train....
The fatal mistress hoists her silken sails,
And shrinking from the fight, invokes the gales.
Aghast she looks, and heaves her breast for breath,
Panting and pale with fear of future death.
The god had figured her as driven along
By winds and waves, and scudding through the throng.
Just opposite, sad Nilus opens wide
His arms and ample bosom to the tide,
And spreads his mantle o'er the winding coast,
In which he wraps the queen and hides the flying host.
The victor to the gods his thanks expressed,
And Rome triumphant with his presence blessed....
Great Caesar sits sublime upon his throne,
Before Apollo's porch of Parian stone,
Accepts the presents vowed for victory,
And hangs the monumental crowns on high....

Virgil,
Aeneid, Book VIII, 30–19 BCE

The battle of Actium

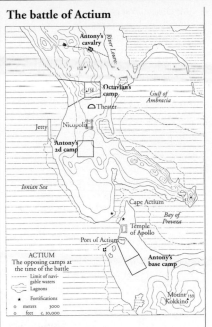

ACTIUM
The opposing camps at
the time of the battle

----- Limit of navi-
gable waters

Lagoons

★ Fortifications

o   meters   3000
o   feet   c. 10,000

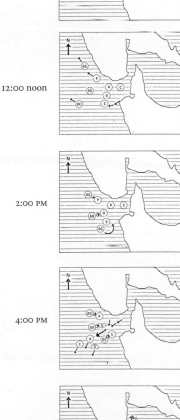

9:00 AM
12:00 noon

12:00 noon

2:00 PM

4:00 PM

Evening

The blockade
The 240 ships of Antony and Cleopatra
cannot reach the open sea, blocked by
Octavian's fleet of 406 ships. Until midday
the adversaries remain stationary.

The engagement
Agrippa feints a retreat. Pursued by Publicola,
he turns sharply about, attacking and
scattering Antony's fleet.

The retreat
Passing through a breach in the enemy line,
Cleopatra reaches the open sea.

Octavian's fleet
AG Marcus Agrippa
AR Lucius Arruntius
OC Octavian

Antony's fleet
A   Mark Antony
O   Marcus Octavius
S   Gaius Sosius
P   Gellius Publicola
C   Cleopatra

A queen of literature

Over the centuries, many of the world's greatest authors have turned to the story of Cleopatra, retelling and coloring it according to their temperaments and times. Like the ancient writers, later poets and biographers have judged the queen both harshly and with sympathy.

Giovanni Boccaccio (1313–75), the great medieval author of witty romances, sonnets, and biographies, places Cleopatra with Eve, Venus, Minerva, and other renowned women of mythology in his collection Concerning Famous Women. *He does not, however, much admire her; an Italian, he favors Rome. Drawing on the ancient sources, he adds several vivid touches of his own to the famous tale.*

CLEOPATRA, QUEEN OF EGYPT

Cleopatra was an Egyptian woman who became an object of gossip for the whole world. Although she was the descendant of Ptolemy, the son of Lagus and king of Macedonia, through a long line of kings,…she nevertheless came to rule through crime. She gained glory for almost nothing else than her beauty, while on the other hand she became known throughout the world for her greed, cruelty and lustfulness.

…Cleopatra, burning with the desire to rule, as some say, poisoned the innocent fifteen-year-old boy who was both her brother and her husband, and ruled the kingdom alone.…

When Caesar arrived in Egypt… armed with wiles and great self-confidence, Cleopatra arrived in royal splendor. Thinking that she would obtain her kingdom if she could draw Caesar, the conqueror of the world, into lustfulness, and being very beautiful and captivating anyone she desired with her shining eyes and her eloquence, with little trouble she brought the lustful prince to her embraces. For many nights she stayed with him among the tumult of the people of Alexandria, and, as almost everyone agrees, she conceived a son, whom she later called Caesarion after his father.

Finally young Ptolemy, abandoned by Caesar and urged on by his men, turned his arms against his liberator… [but] he was defeated by Caesar…. Almost as if he owed her payment for her crime, and because she had been loyal, Caesar gave the kingdom of Egypt to Cleopatra, who desired nothing else. But first he removed her sister Arsinoë, lest she should lead new uprisings against him.

Thus Cleopatra, having already acquired her kingdom through two crimes, gave herself to her pleasures. Having become almost the prostitute of Oriental kings, and greedy for gold and jewels, she not only stripped her lovers of these things with her art, but it was also said that she emptied the temples

A painting by Wertheimer, representing the meeting of Antony and Cleopatra at Tarsus, envisions the scene as one of operatic grandeur, complete with sea nymphs.

and the sacred places of the Egyptians of their vases, statues, and other treasures. Later,…she went to meet [Antony] and easily ensnared that lustful man with her beauty and wanton eyes. She kept him wretchedly in love with her and to remove all threats to her rule, she, who had poisoned her brother, made Antony kill her [other sister] in the temple of the Ephesian Diana, where the unfortunate girl had fled for safety. Cleopatra received this from her new lover as the first reward of her adultery. The wicked woman, already knowing Antony's character, did not fear to ask him for the kingdoms of Syria and Arabia. It seemed to him that this was a serious and unseemly thing; nevertheless, to satisfy the desire of the woman he loved, he gave her a small piece of both countries. And he added also all the cities which are near the Syrian shore between Egypt and the river

Eleutherus, keeping Sidon and Tyre for himself. Having obtained these things, Cleopatra followed Antony all the way to the Euphrates.… Returning to Egypt through Syria, she was received magnificently by Herod Antipater, who at that time was king of Judaea. She was not ashamed to send messengers to him to bring him to her embraces, so that, if he accepted, she could take as payment the kingdom he had gained shortly before through Antony. Realizing this, Herod not only refused through respect for Antony, but to free him from the shame of such a lewd woman he planned to kill her with his sword, but his friends dissuaded him. After failing in her real purpose, Cleopatra, as though she had stopped for this reason, gave Herod the revenue from Jericho.…

Antony had treacherously seized the king of Armenia,…had taken vast treasures from him and was bringing him along shackled with silver chains. To bring covetous Cleopatra to his embraces, effeminate Antony gave her, as she approached, the captive king in all his regalia, as well as the booty. The greedy woman, happy at the gifts, embraced the ardent man so seductively that he made her his wife with great love, after repudiating [his wife] Octavia, the sister of Octavian Caesar. I shall not discuss the Arabian ointments, the perfumes of Saba, and the drunken revels. As Antony gluttonously stuffed himself contin-

The meeting of Antony and Cleopatra at Tarsus has captured the imagination of many artists. Below: a 19th-century engraving.

uously with delicacies, he asked what magnificent thing could be added to the daily banquets, as if he wanted to make his dinners for Cleopatra more splendid. The lewd woman answered that if he wanted she could have a dinner costing more than one hundred thousand sesterces....

As the insatiable woman's craving for kingdoms grew day by day, to grasp everything at once she asked Antony for the Roman empire. Perhaps drunk or rising from such a noble supper, Antony, who was not in full possession of his mental faculties, without properly considering his own strength or the power of the Romans, promised to give it to her, as if it were his to give. Good Lord, how great was the audacity of the woman who requested this! And the madness of the man who promised it was no less! How generous was this man who so rashly gave away to an entreating woman an empire which had just been gained after so many centuries, with such difficulty and bloodshed, through the death of so many great men and even peoples, and with so many noble deeds and battles, as if he wanted to give it away at once like the ownership of a single house!...For this reason war broke out after both sides had gathered their forces. Antony and Cleopatra proceeded to Epirus with their fleet adorned with gold and purple sails.... [At Actium Octavian] attacked them with a great fleet and marvelous daring. When battle had been joined, Mars kept the result in doubt for a long time. Finally, when Antony's forces seemed to be succumbing, proud Cleopatra was the first to flee on her golden ship with sixty other vessels. Antony lowered the ensign of his praetorian

ship and immediately followed her.

...The conqueror Octavian followed them and destroyed their power in several victorious battles. They asked for last minute peace terms. Unable to obtain them, Antony despaired, and, according to some, entered the royal mausoleum, where he killed himself with his sword. When Alexandria had been captured, Cleopatra tried in vain with her old wiles to make young Octavian desire her, as she had done with Caesar and Antony. Angry at hearing that she was being reserved for the conqueror's triumph, and without hope of safety, Cleopatra, dressed in royal garments, followed her Antony. Lying down next to him, she opened the veins of her arms and put two asps in the openings in order to die. Some say that they cause death in sleep. In this sleep the wretched woman put an end to her greed, her concupiscence, and her life....

Giovanni Boccaccio,
Concerning Famous Women,
c. 1360–74,
trans. by Guido A. Guarino

The English poet Geoffrey Chaucer (c. 1342–1400) was much influenced by Boccaccio. But unlike the Italian his political sympathies are not with the ancient Roman empire. He esteems Cleopatra as a woman faithful to love, and writes well of her in The Legend of Good Women, *a series of stories about praiseworthy women of history.*

THE LEGEND OF CLEOPATRA

After the death of the king Ptolemy, who had all Egypt under his rule, Cleopatra his queen reigned; until on a time it befell that out of Rome there was sent a senator to win kingdoms and honors for the town of Rome, as was their wont, that she might have the world under her obedience; and in sooth his name was Antony. As Fortune owed him a disgrace after he had met with prosperity, it so befell that he became a rebel to the town of Rome; and moreover he falsely deserted the sister of Caesar, ere she was aware, and at any cost would have another wife. Wherefore he fell at odds with Caesar and with Rome.

Nevertheless this same senator was a full worthy, noble warrior, in sooth, and his death was full great pity. But Love had brought this man into such a madness and so tightly bound him in his snare, all for love of Cleopatra, that he set all the world at no value. Naught seemed to him so needful as to love and serve Cleopatra. He recked not to die in arms in defence of her and of her right. Eke this noble queen in like fashion loved this knight, for his merit and his knighthood; and certainly, unless the books lie, he was of his person and nobility and discretion and hardiness worthy of any wight alive. And she was as fair as the rose in May. And (for it is best to write briefly) she became his wife and had him as she desired.

To describe the wedding and the festival were too long for me, who have undertaken such an emprise as to put in verses so many stories, lest I should neglect things of greater weight and import. For men may overload a ship or a barge. Therefore I will skip lightly to the conclusion, and let slide all the remnant.

Octavian, maddened by this deed, raised an host of stout Romans, cruel as lions, to lead against Antony for his utter destruction. They went to ship, and I leave them sailing thus. Antony was wary and would not omit to encounter these Romans if he could; he laid his plans, and on a day both he and his wife and all his host went forth anon to ship; they tarried no longer. Out at sea it befell the foes to meet; the trumpet sounds on high, they shout and shoot and at sunrise make fierce onset. With grisly sound out flies the huge shot, and furiously they hurtle together, and from the fore-tops down come the great stones. In amongst the ropes go shearing-hooks and grapnels full of claws. This man and that press on with poleaxes; one flees behind the mast, and out again, and drives the other overboard. One pierces another upon his spear-point; one cuts the sail with hooks like scythes; another brings the wine-cup and bids them be glad; one pours peas upon the hatches to make them slippery; they rush together with pots full of quicklime. And thus they pass the long day in battle, till at last (as everything has an end) Antony is defeated and put to flight, and all his folk scatter as best they can.

The queen with all her purple sails fled likewise from the blows that went thick as hail-stones; no wonder she could not endure it. And when Antony saw that chance he said, 'Alas the day that I was born! So on this day I have lost all mine honor!'; and in despair he started out of his wits, and rove himself to the heart forthwith, ere he went further from the place.

His wife, who could get no mercy from Caesar, fled to Egypt in dread and anguish. But hearken, ye that speak of devotion, ye men who falsely swear by many an oath that ye will die if your beloved be but angered, behold what womanly faithfulness ye may here see. This woful Cleopatra made such lament that no tongue can tell it; but in the morning she would tarry no longer and caused her skillful workmen make a shrine out of all the rubies and fine gems that she could spy out in all Egypt and she filled the shrine with spices and had the body embalmed, and fetched forth this dead corse and enclosed it in the shrine. And next the shrine she had a pit dug, and put therein all the serpents she could find, and thus she spake: 'Now, beloved, whom my sorrowful heart so far obeyed that, from that blissful hour when I swore to be all freely thine,—I mean thee, Antony, my knight—, thou were never out of mine heart's remembrance so long as I was awake, day or night, were it in weal or woe, in the carol or the dance. And then I made this covenant with myself, that, whatever it were thou feltest, weal or woe, the same would I feel, life or death, if it lay in my power for the honor of my wifehood. And that covenant, whilst breath remains in me, I will fulfill; and this shall men see well, never was queen truer to her love.'

And at that word with right good heart she leapt naked into the pit amongst the serpents, and there she chose to be buried. Anon the serpents began to sting her, and she received her death cheerfully, for the love of Antony who was so dear to her. And this is truth of history, it is no fable.

Now, until I find a man thus faithful and steadfast, who will so willingly die for love, I pray God may our heads never ache!

Geoffrey Chaucer,
The Legend of Good Women,
c. 1372–86,
modern English rendition
by John S. P. Tatlock

William Shakespeare (1564–1616), in Antony and Cleopatra, *as in other tragedies, shows a woman's passion as not only noble, but ennobling. Here the two lovers meet for the last time.*

CLEOPATRA: O sun,
Burn the great sphere thou mov'st in, darkling stand
The varying shore o' th' world! O Antony,
Antony, Antony! Help, Charmian, help, Iras, help:
Help, friends below, let's draw him hither.
ANTONY: Peace!
Not Caesar's valor hath o'erthrown Antony,
But Antony's hath triumphed on itself.
CLEOPATRA: So it should be, that none but Antony
Should conquer Antony, but woe 'tis so!
ANTONY: I am dying, Egypt, dying; only
I here importune death awhile, until
Of many thousand kisses the poor last
I lay upon thy lips.
CLEOPATRA: I dare not, dear;
Dear my lord, pardon; I dare not,
Lest I be taken. Not th' imperious show
of the full-fortuned Caesar ever shall
Be brooched with me, if knife, drugs, serpents have
Edge, sting, or operation. I am safe:
Your wife Octavia, with her modest eyes
And still conclusion, shall acquire no honor
Demuring upon me. But come, come, Antony!
Help me, my women, we must draw thee up:
Assist, good friends.

ANTONY: O, quick, or I am gone.
CLEOPATRA: Here's sport indeed! How
heavy weighs my lord!
Our strength is all gone into heaviness:
That makes the weight. Had I great
Juno's power,
The strong-winged Mercury should
fetch thee up
And set thee by Jove's side. Yet come
a little,
Wishers were ever fools. O, come,
come, come.
They heave Antony aloft to Cleopatra.
And welcome, welcome! Die when thou
hast lived,
Quicken with kissing. Had my lips that
power,
Thus would I wear them out.

P oster from the 1934 film *Cleopatra,* starring
Claudette Colbert.

ALL: A heavy sight!
ANTONY: I am dying, Egypt, dying.
Give me some wine and let me speak
a little.
CLEOPATRA: No, let me speak, and let
me rail so high
That the false huswife Fortune break
her wheel,
Provoked by my offense.
ANTONY: One word, sweet queen.
Of Caesar seek your honor, with your
safety. O!
CLEOPATRA: They do not go together.
William Shakespeare,
Antony and Cleopatra,
IV, xv, c. 1607

*The tragedies of the playwright Pierre
Corneille (1606–84) are among the
greatest in French literature. In* The
Death of Pompey *Cleopatra is a savvy
ruler measuring the rising and falling
fortunes of other rulers, and negotiating
with them.*

CLEOPATRA: …My Charmian, [Caesar]
comes here within our walls
To seek me as his battles' prize,—
to lay
All of his glory at my feet and make
Subject to my decree that heart and
hand
Which rule great kings; and a rejection
by me,
If mingled now with his campaign's
success,
Would leave earth's master reft of
happiness!
CHARMIAN: I well might dare to take
oath that thy charms
Boast of a pow'r which they will not
employ,
And mighty Caesar will have naught
to vex him
If thy disdain alone can mar his fortunes.

But what does thou expect, to what
aspirest thou,
Since he already is another's
husband, —
Since an untroubled marriage with
Calpurnia
Holdeth his spirit bound by sacred
bonds?

CLEOPATRA: Divorce is common now
among the Romans
And can remove for me these obstacles.
Caesar knows well its practice and
procedure:
It made room in his own home for
Calpurnia.

CHARMIAN: He might in the same way
abandon thee.

CLEOPATRA: Good fortune may be mine
to hold him better.
My lover perhaps will have advantages
By which I somehow can retain his
heart.
But let us leave to chance whate'er may
come,
And make this marriage if it can be
made.
Though it should last for but one day,
my glory
Will be unrivaled, for I shall become
At least for one day mistress of the
world.
I have ambition, and be it vice or virtue
My heart will 'neath its load be gladly
broken.
I love its fervency and will ever call it
The only passion worthy of a princess.
But I wish honor to incite its ardor
and lead me without shame to lofty
greatness;
And I would disavow it, should its
madness
Offer to me a throne dishonorably....
But here is good Acoreus, come back,
From whom I shall learn certain news
of him....

*Enter ACOREUS [who describes the
death of Pompey at the hands of Caesar's
minions, Septimius and Achillas].*

ACOREUS: ...[And now] Caesar is in
another quarter spied
Coming from Thessaly; a fleet is seen
Whose numbers one could scarcely
count....

CLEOPATRA: 'Tis he
Himself, Acoreus; that is beyond
doubt.
Quake, quake, ye miscreants; here is
heaven's thunder.
Means have I now to grind you into
dust!
Caesar comes; I am queen; Pompey
hath vengeance;
Tyranny is brought low; Fate's course is
changed.
But let us marvel at great men's
destinies,
Pity them, and by them judge what we
are.
That general of a senate the world's
master,
Whose prosperous lot appeared above
disaster,
He whom Rome saw, more feared than
bolts of lightning,
Thrice triumph, in three regions of the
earth,
And who in his last battles still beheld
Both consuls alike following his
banners—
No sooner doth calamity attend him
Than Egypt's monsters can ordain his
fate.
One then sees an Achillas, a Septimius,
And a Photinus suddenly become
The sovereign arbiters of his noble
fortunes.
A king who from his hands received his
crown
Basely abandons him to these Court-
vermin.

Thus endeth Pompey; and perchance someday
Caesar may meet his end in the same way.
Make false my augury, gods, who see my tears!
Favor my heart's prayers and his conquering spears!

CHARMIAN: Madam, the King is coming. He may hear thee.

Enter PTOLEMY.

PTOLEMY: Knowest thou the happiness we are to enjoy,
My sister?

CLEOPATRA: Yes, I know; Caesar is here;
I am no more a prisoner of Photinus.

PTOLEMY: Wouldst thou hate ever this faithful subject?

François Chauveau, *The Death of Pompey,* a 1644 engraving illustrating the play by Pierre Corneille.

LA. MORT. DE. POMPEE.
A. PARIS.
Chez. A. De. Sommaville. & A. Courbe.

CLEOPATRA: No;
But I, now being free, laugh at his plans.

PTOLEMY: What plans had he of which thou couldst complain?

CLEOPATRA: I suffered much from them,—had more to fear.
So great a schemer would do anything,
And thou to all he counseled gavest ear.

PTOLEMY: If I have followed his advice,
I knew its wisdom.

CLEOPATRA: If I dreaded the results,
I knew its ruthlessness.

PTOLEMY: For his realm's welfare,
Everything that a king may do is just.

CLEOPATRA: This kind of justice is for me to fear....

PTOLEMY: ...I can now to this triumphant conqueror [Caesar]
Safely offer my kingdom and thy heart.

CLEOPATRA: I can make *my* gifts; see thou but to thine,
And with thy interests do not confound mine.

PTOLEMY: Thine are mine own, we being of one blood.

CLEOPATRA: Thou canst say, too, "We having the same rank,
Being alike sovereigns"; and yet I think
There are some differences between our interests....

Pierre Corneille,
The Death of Pompey,
1643,
trans. by Lacy Lockert

The English poet John Dryden (1631–1700) translated many of the ancient texts describing the queen of Egypt; his drama All for Love *portrays the military and amorous dilemmas of the lovers.*

SERAPION: How stands the queen affected?

ALEXAS: Oh, she dotes,
She dotes, Serapion, on this vanquished man,
And winds herself about his mighty ruins;
Whom would she yet forsake, yet yield him up,
This hunted prey, to his pursuer's hands,
She might preserve us all; but 'tis in vain....

[*Later*]

ANTONY: I have never used
My soldiers to demand a reason of
My actions. Why did they refuse to march?
VENTIDIUS: They said they would not fight for Cleopatra.
ANTONY: What was't they said?
VENTIDIUS: They said they would not fight for Cleopatra.
Why should they fight, indeed, to make her conquer,
And make you more a slave? to gain you kingdoms,
Which, for a kiss at your next midnight feast,
You'll sell to her? Then she new-names her jewels,
And calls this diamond such or such a tax;
Each pendant in her ear shall be a province.
ANTONY: Ventidius, I allow your tongue free license
On all my other faults; but on your life,
No word of Cleopatra. She deserves
More worlds than I can lose....

[*Later again*]

CLEOPATRA: I will come.
Doubt not, my life, I'll come, and quickly too:
Caesar shall triumph o'er no part of thee.

ANTONY: But grieve not, while thou stay'st
My last disastrous times:
Think we have had a clear and glorious day,
And heav'n did kindly to delay the storm
Just till our close of ev'ning. Ten years' love,
And not a moment lost, but all improved
To th'utmost joys—what ages have we lived!
And now to die each other's; and so dying,
While hand in hand we walk in groves below,
Whole troops of lovers' ghosts shall flock about us,
And all the train be ours....

[*Later again*]

CHARMION: Remember, madam,
He charged you not to grieve.
CLEOPATRA: And I'll obey him.
I have not loved a Roman not to know
What should become his wife—his wife, my Charmion!
For 'tis to that high title I aspire,
And now I'll not die less. Let dull Octavia
Survive, to mourn him dead; my nobler fate
Shall knit our spousals with a tie too strong
For Roman laws to break.
IRAS: Will you then die?
CLEOPATRA: Why shouldst thou make that question?
IRAS: Caesar is merciful.
CLEOPATRA: Let him be so
To those that want his mercy....

John Dryden,
All for Love,
1677

In the play Caesar and Cleopatra *Bernard Shaw (1856–1950) focuses upon the difference in age between the grizzled Roman general and the young, untried queen. At the beginning of this passage, Cleopatra does not know she is speaking to the ruler of Rome.*

CAESAR: Caesar never eats women.
CLEOPATRA: (*springing up full of hope*) What!
CAESAR: (*impressively*) But he eats girls (*she relapses*) and cats. Now you are a silly little girl; and you are descended from the black kitten. You are both a girl and a cat.
CLEOPATRA: (*trembling*) And will he eat me?
CAESAR: Yes, unless you make him believe that you are a woman.
CLEOPATRA: Oh, you must get a sorcerer to make a woman of me. Are you a sorcerer?
CAESAR: Perhaps. But it will take a long time; and this very night you must stand face to face with Caesar in the palace of your fathers.
CLEOPATRA: No, no. I darent.
CAESAR: Whatever dread may be in your soul—however terrible Caesar may be to you—you must confront him as a brave woman and a great queen; and you must feel no fear. If your hand shakes: if your voice quavers; then— night and death! (*She moans*). But if he thinks you worthy to rule, he will set you on the throne by his side and make you the real ruler of Egypt....
CLEOPATRA: Oh please, please! I will do whatever you tell me. I will be good. I will be your slave....

Later, Caesar shows Cleopatra how to establish her authority over a presumptuous handmaiden. Cleopatra is intoxi-cated with the discovery of her power.

CLEOPATRA: ...I am a real Queen at last—a real, real Queen! Cleopatra the Queen! (*Caesar shakes his head dubiously, the advantage of the change seeming open to question from the point of view of the general welfare of Egypt....*) Oh, I love you for making me a queen.
CAESAR: But queens love only kings.
CLEOPATRA: I will make all the men I love kings. I will make you a king. I will have many young kings, with round, strong arms; and when I am tired of them I will whip them to death; but you shall always be my king: my nice, kind, wise, good old king.
CAESAR: Oh, my wrinkles, my wrinkles! And my child's heart! You will be the most dangerous of all Caesar's conquests....

Bernard Shaw,
Caesar and Cleopatra, 1900

In his bitter satire The Threepenny Opera *Bertolt Brecht (1898–1956) used Cleopatra and Caesar as examples of the universality of human experience—the more things change, the more they stay the same:*

THE SONG OF SOLOMON

...You saw Queen Cleopatra too
And what her talents were.
Oh, it was quite a life she led
Until her past caught up with her!
Two emperors joined her in bed:
Such goings-on in Babylon!
But long before the day was out
The consequence was clear, alas!
Her very beauty brought her to this pass:
A woman's better off without.

And Julius Caesar: he was brave.
His fame shall never cease.
He sat like God on an altarpiece

And then they tore him limb from limb
And Brutus helped to slaughter him.
Old Julius was very brave
But long before the day was out
The consequence was clear, alas!
His bravery 'twas that brought him to
    this pass:
A man is better off without.

You know the inquisitive Bertolt Brecht.

In this charming if anachronistic engraving Cleopatra kills herself in 18th-century dress while her two servants look on.

His songs—you loved them so.
But when too oft he asked where from
The riches of the rich did come
You made him pack his bag and go.
Oh how inquisitive was Brecht!
But long before the day was out
The consequence was clear, alas!
Inquisitiveness had brought him to this
    pass:
A man is better off without....

Bertolt Brecht,
The Threepenny Opera, III, i,
1928,
trans. by Eric Bentley

Orientalism

To classical Greek and Roman authors Cleopatra was a "perverse" Eastern monster—exotic and dangerous. When Napoleon conquered Egypt in 1799, bringing large collections of art back to Paris, 19th-century Europeans reacted with the same mixture of suspicion and fascination. A taste for Egyptian-revival styles in dress, furniture, and the arts swept the fashionable world. As the British and French empires exposed Westerners to the East, artists and writers interpreted the Orient as a culture of sensuality, luxury, decadence, and mystery. Cleopatra, naturally, played a leading role in Orientalist work, whose sources remained the ancient descriptions.

Barbarous splendor

Plutarch describes the fateful meeting between Cleopatra and Antony at Tarsus in grandiose language. This scene has been reproduced in countless plays, films, and paintings.

She came sailing up the river Cydnus, in a barge with gilded stern and outspread sails of purple, while oars of silver beat time to the music of flutes and fifes and harps. She herself lay all along under a canopy of cloth of gold, dressed as Venus in a picture, and beautiful young boys, like painted Cupids, stood on each side to fan her. Her maids were dressed like sea-nymphs and graces, some steering at the rudder, some working at the ropes. The perfumes diffused themselves from the vessel to the shore.

Plutarch,
"Life of Antony," 1st–2d century CE

Lucan's equally lavish description of a sumptuous feast that Cleopatra served to Julius Caesar was irresistibly splendid to later writers.

The purchase of Caesar's favour at so high a price had, of course, to be celebrated with a banquet, and a tremendous bustle arose when she appeared in her full magnificence—this being before Roman society had adopted degenerate Eastern fashions. Her banqueting hall was as large as a temple, and more luxurious than even our present corrupt age could easily imitate. Its fretted ceilings were encrusted with precious stones, and its rafters heavily plated with gold. The walls were marble, not merely marble-faced; pillars of sheer agate and porphyry supported the roof; and the entire palace had an onyx pavement. Similarly, the great door-posts were solid ebony, not common timber with an ebony veneer; these costly materials, in effect, served a functional, not merely a decorative, purpose. The entrance hall was panelled in ivory, and its doors inlaid with tinted tortoise-shell, the dark patches concealed by emeralds. There were jewel-studded couches, rows of yellow jasper wine-cups on the tables, bright coverlets spread over the sofas—mostly Tyrian purple repeatedly dyed, and either embroidered in gold, or shot with fiery threads of cochineal in Egyptian style. As for the courtiers and the palace staff, what an assemblage they made: old, and young, and of such various pigmentation! Some had black Numidian hair, some hair so blond that Caesar swore he had never seen the like even in the Rhinelands; others were Negroes,

Louis-Marie Baader, *The Death of Cleopatra*, a 19th-century Orientalist painting.

notable for dusky skins.... One group consisted of unfortunate boys, lately castrated; and opposite them stood a somewhat elder generation of eunuchs, almost as beardless as they.

In this royal banqueting hall Caesar reclined, a power above all kings, and Cleopatra beside him. Neither her sceptre nor her marriage now contented her, and she had added the finishing touches to an already fatal beauty by putting on so many wreaths and neck-laces of Red Sea pearls, that she posi-tively panted under their weight. Her white breasts showed through the Chinese silk which, though closely woven when imported, had been teased out by some Egyptian mercer until it became diaphanous. The tables were rounds of citrus-wood, supported on gleaming elephant tusks—Caesar never saw anything so fine even after his conquest of King Juba....

Every variety of flesh, fowl, sea-fish or river-fish, every delicacy that extrava-gance, prompted not by hunger but by

a mad love of ostentation, could rout out from the ends of the earth, came served on golden dishes. Cleopatra went so far as to offer Caesar birds and beasts which the Egyptians held sacred; and provided Nile water in ewers of rock crystal for washing his hands. The wine in those huge jewelled goblets was of no local vintage, but a Falernian fetched from Italy, which though a little rough when first casked, becomes nobly mellowed after a few years of careful cellarage at Meroë in Upper Egypt. Each guest had received wreaths of flowering spikenard and perpetual roses, and the fresh oil of cinnamon which they poured on their hair had lost none of its fragrance in transit from the East; and to this they added oil of cardamum recently imported....

Lucan,
Civil War, Book X, c. 62 CE

The painter S. Daynes-Grassot depicts *Cleopatra Testing Her Poisons on Her Slaves.*

Deadlier than the male

The Russian poet Aleksandr Sergeyevich Pushkin (1799–1837) wrote an "improvisation" on Lucan's theme in an unfinished short story, from which these lines are taken.

The palace shone. Sweet songs resounded
To lyres and flutes. The dazzling queen
With voice and look inspired the feasters
And kindled the resplendent scene;
Her throne drew all men's hearts and
    glances,
But suddenly her fervor fled;
Pensive, she held her golden goblet,
And o'er it bent her wondrous head....
The regal feast seems hushed in slumber,
The guests, the choir, are still. But she
now lifts her head up to address them
With an assured serenity:
"My love brings bliss...."

Aleksandr Sergeyevich Pushkin,
Egyptian Nights,
1835,
trans. by T. Keane and
Babette Deutsch

L eontyne Price as the queen in the 1966 Metropolitan Opera (New York) production of Samuel
Barber's *Antony and Cleopatra.*

Poisoned love

The French writer Théophile Gautier (1811–72) portrays Cleopatra in a cruel and disturbing light, in the best Romantic Orientalist style.

"Ah," continued Cleopatra, "I wish that something would happen to me, some strange, unexpected adventure. The songs of the poets; the dances of the Syrian slaves; the banquets, rose

In 1829 the French Romantic composer Hector Berlioz wrote a lyrical scene on the theme of the death of Cleopatra. Below and opposite: the opening passages.

Kleopatra.
Lyrische Scene.
Deutsche Übersetzung von Emma Klingenfeld.

Cléopâtre.
Scène Lyrique.
Poème de P. A. Vieillard.

Cleopatra.
Lyric Scene.
English Translation by John Bernhoff.

H. Berlioz.
Componirt in Paris Juli 1829.

garlanded, and prolonged into the dawn; the nocturnal races; the Laconian dogs; the tame lions...the clusters of pearls; the perfumes from Asia; the most exquisite of luxuries; the wildest of splendors—nothing any longer gives me pleasure. Everything is insupportable to me."

"It is easy to be seen," muttered Charmion to herself, "that the queen has not had a lover nor had anyone killed for a whole month."

...The orgie was at its height: the dishes of phenicopters' [flamingoes'] tongues, and the livers of scarus fish; the eels fattened upon human flesh,

and cooked in brine; the dishes of peacock's brains; the boars stuffed with living birds; and all the marvels of the antique banquets were heaped upon the three table-surfaces of the gigantic triclinium. The wines of Crete, of Massicus, and of Falernus foamed up in cratera wreathed with roses, and filled by Asian pages whose beautiful flowing hair served the guests to wipe their hands upon. Musicians playing upon the sistrum, the tympanum, the sambuke, and the harp with one-and-twenty strings filled all the upper galleries, and mingled their harmonies with the tempest of sound that hovered over the feast. Even the deep-voiced thunder could not have made itself heard there.

Meïamoun, whose head was lying on Cleopatra's shoulder, felt as though his reason were leaving him. The banquet-hall whirled around him like a vast architectural nightmare; through the dizzy glare he beheld perspectives and colonnades without end; new zones of porticoes seemed to uprear themselves upon the real fabric, and bury their summits in heights of sky to which Babel never rose. Had he not felt within his hand the soft, cool hand of Cleopatra, he would have believed himself transported into an enchanted world by some witch of Thessaly or Magian of Persia.

Toward the close of the repast humpbacked dwarfs and mummers engaged in grotesque dances and combats; then young Egyptian and Greek maidens, representing the black and white Hours, danced with inimitable grace a voluptuous dance after the Ionian manner.

Cleopatra herself arose from her throne, threw aside her royal mantle, replaced her starry diadem with a garland of flowers, attached golden *crotali* [finger-cymbals] to her alabaster hands, and began to dance before Meïamoun, who was ravished with delight. Her beautiful arms, rounded like the handles of an alabaster vase, shook out bunches of sparkling notes, and her *crotali* prattled with ever-increasing volubility. Poised on the pink tips of her little feet, she approached swiftly to graze the forehead of Meïamoun with a kiss; then she recommenced her wondrous art, and flitted around him, now backward-leaning, with head reversed, eyes half closed, arms lifelessly relaxed, locks uncurled and loose-hanging like a Bacchante of Mount Maenalus; now again, active, animated, laughing, fluttering, more tireless and capricious in her movements than the pilfering bee. Heart-consuming love, sensual pleasure, burning passion, youth inexhaustible and ever-fresh, the promise of bliss to come—she expressed all....

The modest stars had ceased to contemplate the scene; their golden eyes could not endure such a spectacle; the heaven itself was blotted out, and a dome of flaming vapor covered the hall.

Cleopatra seated herself once more by Meïamoun. Night advanced; the last of the black Hours was about to take flight; a faint blue glow entered with bewildered aspect into the tumult of ruddy light as a moonbeam falls into a furnace; the upper arcades became suffused with pale azure tints—day was breaking.

Meïamoun took the horn vase which an Ethiopian slave of sinister countenance presented to him, and which contained a poison so violent that it would have caused any other vase to

burst asunder. Flinging his whole life to
his mistress in one last look, he lifted
to his lips the fatal cup in which the
envenomed liquor boiled up, hissing.

Cleopatra turned pale, and laid her
hand on Meïamoun's arm to stay the
act. His courage touched her. She was
about to say, "Live to love me yet, I
desire it!..." when the sound of a
clarion was heard. Four heralds-at-arms
entered the banquet-hall on horseback;
they were officers of Mark Antony, and
rode but a short distance in advance of
their master. Cleopatra silently loosened
the arm of Meïamoun. A long ray of
sunlight suddenly played upon her
forehead, as though trying to replace
her absent diadem.

"You see the moment has come; it is
daybreak, it is the hour when happy
dreams take flight," said Meïamoun.
Then he emptied the fatal vessel at a
draught, and fell as though struck by
lightning. Cleopatra bent her head, and
one burning tear—the only one she had
ever shed—fell into her cup to mingle
with the molten pearl.

"By Hercules, my fair queen! I made
all speed in vain. I see I have come too
late," cried Mark Antony, entering the
banquet-hall, "the supper is over. But
what signifies this corpse upon the
pavement?"

"Oh, nothing!" returned Cleopatra,
with a smile; "only a poison I was
testing with the idea of using it upon
myself should Augustus take me
prisoner. My dear Lord, will you not
please to take a seat beside me, and
watch those Greek buffoons dance?"

Théophile Gautier,
"One of Cleopatra's Nights," from
*One of Cleopatra's Nights and
Other Fantastic Romances,* 1838,
trans. by Lafcadio Hearn

The princess and the soldier

*Gustave Flaubert (1821–80) traveled in
Egypt in the first half of the 19th century.
His description of the Carthaginian
princess Salammbô, in the novel of the
same name, owes a great deal to ancient
authors—like Plutarch's Cleopatra she
speaks many languages, and like Lucan
Flaubert lingers over the opulent, sensual
splendor of his scene.*

The [soldiers] commenced to drink
again. Their ragged tunics were wet
with the perfumes that flowed in large
drops from their foreheads, and resting
both fists on the tables, which seemed
to them to be rocking like ships, they
rolled their great drunken eyes around
to devour by sight what they could not
take. Others walked amid the dishes on
the purple table covers, breaking ivory
stools and phials of Tyrian glass to
pieces with their feet. Songs mingled
with the death-rattle of the slaves
expiring amid the broken cups. They
demanded wine, meat, gold. They cried
out for women. They raved in a
hundred languages.... The clamour
redoubled; the wounded lions roared
in the shade.

In an instant the highest terrace of
the palace was illuminated, the central
door opened, and a woman, Hamilcar's
daughter herself, clothed in black
garments, appeared on the threshold.
... Motionless and with head bent, she
gazed upon the soldiers.

Her hair, which was powdered with
violet sand, and combined into the
form of a tower, after the fashion of
the Chanaanite maidens, added to
her height. Tresses of pearls were
fastened to her temples, and fell to
the corners of her mouth, which was as

rosy as a half-open pomegranate. On her breast was a collection of luminous stones, their variegation imitating the scales of the murena. Her arms were adorned with diamonds, and issued naked from her sleeveless tunic, which was starred with red flowers on a perfectly black ground. Between her ankles she wore a golden chainlet to regulate her steps, and her large dark purple mantle, cut of an unknown material, trailed behind her, making, as it were, at each step, a broad wave which followed her....

With a woman's subtlety she was simultaneously employing all the dialects of the Barbarians in order to appease their anger. To the Greeks she spoke Greek; then she turned to the Ligurians, the Campanians, the Negroes, and listening to her each one found again in her voice the sweetness of his native land....

Gustave Flaubert,
Salammbo, 1862,
trans. by J. C. Chartres

"Bring me the head of John the Baptist!"

In the late 19th century, Oscar Wilde (1854–1900) was a leading exponent of an extreme, exhausted aestheticism; his Salomé represents a complete transmutation of the vigorous, passionate materiality of Plutarch's and Lucan's Cleopatra. She is a dead soul, a corrupt virgin whose lust is awakened by John the Baptist's spiritual intensity, and—perhaps—by his own denied desire for her.

THE YOUNG SYRIAN: How pale the Princess is! Never have I seen her so pale. She is like the shadow of a white rose in a mirror of silver.

THE PAGE OF HERODIAS: You must not

look at her. You look too much at her....

THE CAPPADOCIAN: Is that the Queen Herodias, she who wears a black mitre sewed with pearls, and whose hair is powdered with blue dust?

FIRST SOLDIER: Yes; that is Herodias, the Tetrarch's wife.

SECOND SOLDIER: The Tetrarch is very fond of wine. He has wine of three sorts. One which is brought from the Island of Samothrace, and is purple like the cloak of Caesar.

THE CAPPADOCIAN: I have never seen Caesar.

SECOND SOLDIER: Another that comes from a town called Cyprus, and is as yellow as gold.

THE CAPPADOCIAN: I love gold.

SECOND SOLDIER: And the third is a wine of Sicily. That wine is red as blood....

THE YOUNG SYRIAN: You have left the feast, Princess?

SALOMÉ: How sweet is the air here! I can breathe here! Within there are Jews from Jerusalem who are tearing each other in pieces over their foolish ceremonies, and barbarians who drink and drink, and spill their wine on the pavement, and Greeks from Smyrna with painted eyes and painted cheeks, and frizzed hair curled in columns, and Egyptians silent and subtle, with long nails of jade and russet cloaks, and Romans brutal and coarse, with their uncouth jargon. Ah! how I loathe the Romans!

Oscar Wilde,
Salomé, 1894

Opposite: two scenes from the 1963 film. Page 151: the beautiful Vivien Leigh as Cleopatra in the 1945 film *Caesar and Cleopatra*.

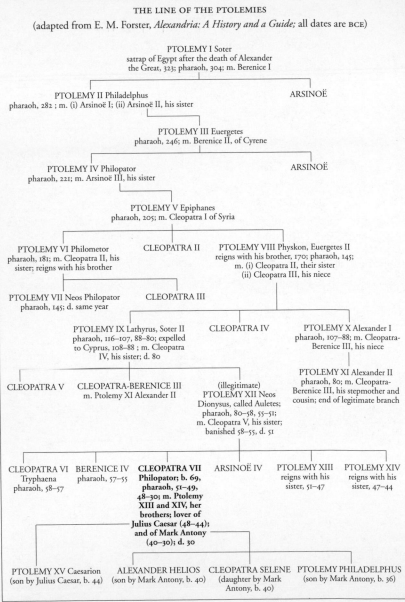

THE LINE OF THE PTOLEMIES
(adapted from E. M. Forster, *Alexandria: A History and a Guide;* all dates are BCE)

PTOLEMY I Soter
satrap of Egypt after the death of Alexander
the Great, 323; pharaoh, 304; m. Berenice I

PTOLEMY II Philadelphus
pharaoh, 282 ; m. (i) Arsinoë I; (ii) Arsinoë II, his sister

ARSINOË

PTOLEMY III Euergetes
pharaoh, 246; m. Berenice II, of Cyrene

PTOLEMY IV Philopator
pharaoh, 221; m. Arsinoë III, his sister

ARSINOË

PTOLEMY V Epiphanes
pharaoh, 205; m. Cleopatra I of Syria

PTOLEMY VI Philometor
pharaoh, 181; m. Cleopatra II, his
sister; reigns with his brother

CLEOPATRA II

PTOLEMY VIII Physkon, Euergetes II
reigns with his brother, 170; pharaoh, 145;
m. (i) Cleopatra II, their sister
(ii) Cleopatra III, his niece

PTOLEMY VII Neos Philopator
pharaoh, 145; d. same year

CLEOPATRA III

PTOLEMY IX Lathyrus, Soter II
pharaoh, 116–107, 88–80; expelled
to Cyprus, 108–88 ; m. Cleopatra
IV, his sister; d. 80

CLEOPATRA IV

PTOLEMY X Alexander I
pharaoh, 107–88; m. Cleopatra-
Berenice III, his niece

PTOLEMY XI Alexander II
pharaoh, 80; m. Cleopatra-
Berenice III, his stepmother and
cousin; end of legitimate branch

CLEOPATRA V

CLEOPATRA-BERENICE III
m. Ptolemy XI Alexander II

(illegitimate)
PTOLEMY XII Neos
Dionysus, called Auletes;
pharaoh, 80–58, 55–51;
m. Cleopatra V, his sister;
banished 58–55, d. 51

CLEOPATRA VI
Tryphaena
pharaoh, 58–57

BERENICE IV
pharaoh, 57–55

**CLEOPATRA VII
Philopator; b. 69,
pharaoh, 51–49,
48–30; m. Ptolemy
XIII and XIV, her
brothers; lover of
Julius Caesar (48–44);
and of Mark Antony
(40–30); d. 30**

ARSINOË IV

PTOLEMY XIII
reigns with his
sister, 51–47

PTOLEMY XIV
reigns with his
sister, 47–44

PTOLEMY XV Caesarion
(son by Julius Caesar, b. 44)

ALEXANDER HELIOS
(son by Mark Antony, b. 40)

CLEOPATRA SELENE
(daughter by Mark
Antony, b. 40)

PTOLEMY PHILADELPHUS
(son by Mark Antony, b. 36)

Chronology

All dates are BCE

106 Birth of Pompey
100 Birth of Julius Caesar
83? Birth of Mark Antony
69 Birth of Cleopatra
63 Birth of Octavian
59 First Triumvirate: Julius Caesar rules with Pompey and Crassus
55 Gabinius restores Ptolemy XII Auletes to the throne of Egypt
51 Cleopatra and Ptolemy XIII rule
49 War between Pompey and Caesar begins;

Cleopatra flees Alexandria
48 Pompey murdered; War of Alexandria; Cleopatra returns to the throne of Egypt, ruling with Cleopatra and Ptolemy XIV
47 Birth of Caesarion
46 Cleopatra is in Rome
44 Caesar is murdered; Cleopatra is in Alexandria
43 Second Triumvirate: Octavian, Mark Antony, and Lepidus rule
42 Battle of Philippi

41 The meeting of Cleopatra and Antony at Tarsus
40 The empire is divided up at Brundisium; Antony marries Octavia
40/39 Birth of Cleopatra and Antony's twins, Alexander Helios and Cleopatra Selene
37 The Triumvirate is renewed; Cleopatra and Antony meet again
36 The war against the Parthians; birth of Ptolemy Philadelphus to

Cleopatra and Antony
34 The "Donations of Alexandria"
32 Antony repudiates Octavia
31 2 September: battle of Actium
30 Deaths of Antony and Cleopatra; Egypt becomes a Roman province
29 Octavian's Triumph at Rome
27 Octavian is given the title Augustus; beginning of the principate

Further Reading

ANCIENT SOURCES

Appian, *The Civil Wars*, Books II–V, trans. H. E. White, 1912–13

Caesar, [Julius], *The Civil Wars*, Books I–III, trans. A. J. Peskett, 1914

Cicero, Marcus Tullius, *Letters to Atticus*, trans. D. R. Shackleton Bailey, 1967; *Philippics*, trans. Walter C. A. Kerr, 1926

Dio Cassius, *Roman History*, trans. Earnest Cary, based on the version of Herbert Baldwin Foster, 1916

Florus, Lucius Annaeus, *Epitome of Roman History*, trans. E. S. Forster, 1929

Gellius, Aulus, *Attic Nights*, trans. J. C. Rolfe, 1927–28

Horace, *Odes; Epodes*, trans. W. G. Shepherd, 1983

Josephus, [Flavius], *Antiquities of the Jews*, Books XIV–XV, trans. Ralph Marcus, 1933, 1963; *The Jewish War*, Book I, trans. H. St. J. Thackeray, 1927

Lucan, *Civil War* (sometimes called *Pharsalia*), trans. Robert Graves, 1957

Pliny the Elder, *Natural History*, Book IX, trans. Philemon Holland, 1601, ed. J. Newsome, 1964

Plutarch, *Lives of the Noble Grecians and Romans [Parallel Lives]*, esp. Lives of Antony, Caesar, Cicero, Brutus, trans. John Dryden, 1683–86, rev. A. H. Clough, 1864

Propertius, Sextus, *Elegies*, trans. G. P. Goold, 1990

Strabo, *The Geography of Strabo*, trans. Horace Leonard Jones, rev. ed. 1967

Suetonius Tranquillus, Gaius, *The Twelve Caesars*, esp. Julius Caesar and Augustus, trans. Robert Graves, 1957, rev. Michael Grant, 1989

Velleius Paterculus, Gaius, *Roman History*, Book II, trans. F. W. Shipley, 1924

Virgil, *Aeneid*, trans. John Dryden, 1697, ed. Howard Clarke, 1989

STUDIES

Balsdon, J. P.V. D., *Roman Women: Their History and Habits*, 1983

Bowman, Alan K., *Egypt after the Pharaohs, 332 BC–AD 642: From Alexander to the Arab Conquest*, 2d ed., 1996

Cambridge Ancient History, vols. IX, X, 1932, 1934

Forster, E. M., *Alexandria: A History and a Guide*, 3d ed., 1960

Franzeno, Carlo Maria, *The Life and Times of Cleopatra*, 1957

Grant, Michael, *Cleopatra: A Biography*, 1972

———, *From Alexander to Cleopatra*, 1990

Green, Peter, *From Alexander to Actium: The Historical Evolution of the Hellenistic Age*, 1990

Gruen, Erich S., *The Hellenistic World and the Coming of Rome*, 1984

Hughes-Hallett, Lucy, *Cleopatra: Histories, Dreams and Distortions*, 1990

Lewis, Naphtali, *Life in Egypt under Roman Rule*, 1983

Meier, Christian, *Julius Caesar*, trans. David McLintock, 1982

Rickett, L. M., *The Administration of Ptolemaic Egypt under Cleopatra VII*, 1980

Trigger, Bruce G., et al., *Ancient Egypt: A Social History*, 1983

Weigall, Arthur, *The Life and Times of Cleopatra*, 1968

List of Illustrations

Key: a=above; *b*=below; *c*=center; *l*=left; *r*=right

Paintings are oil on canvas unless otherwise noted.

Front cover: Jean-André Rixens, *The Death of Cleopatra* (detail), 1874. Musée des Augustins, Toulouse
Spine: Alexandre Cabanel, *Cleopatra Testing Poisons on the Prisoners Condemned to Death* (detail), 1887. Musée Royal des Beaux-Arts, Antwerp
Back cover: Louis-Marie Baader, *The Death of Cleopatra*. Musée des Beaux-Arts, Rennes
1 R. Arthur, *The Suicide of Cleopatra* (detail), 19th century. Roy Miles Fine Paintings, London
2 Guercino (Giovanni Francesco Barbieri), *The Dying Cleopatra* (detail), 1648. Palazzo Rosso, Genoa
3 Guercino, *The Dying Cleopatra* (detail), 1648. Palazzo Rosso, Genoa
4 Antonio Bellucci, *The Death of Cleopatra* (detail), c. 1700. Musée Municipaux, Clermont-Ferrand, France
5 Louis-Jean-François Lagrenée, *The Death of Cleopatra* (detail), 1774. Louvre, Paris
6 Claude Vignon, known as Le Vieux, *The Death of Cleopatra* (detail), c. 1643–57. Musée des

Beaux-Arts, Rennes
7 Guido Reni, *Cleopatra* (detail), 1638–39. Palazzo Pitti, Florence
8 R. Arthur, *The Suicide of Cleopatra* (detail), 19th century. Roy Miles Fine Paintings, London
9 Guido Cagnacci, *The Death of Cleopatra* (detail), 1659–62. Kunsthistorisches Museum, Gemäldegalerie, Vienna
11 Giulio Clovio, after Raphael, *Cleopatra,* drawing, 16th century. Louvre, Cabinet des Dessins, Paris
12 Reconstruction by Johann Bernhard Fischer von Erlach of the Lighthouse of Alexandria, from *Entwurff einer historischen Architectur*, 1725
13 Alexandrian tinted glass. Greco-Roman Museum, Alexandria
14a Alexandrian coin, period of Ptolemy I, 4th century BCE. Bibliothèque Nationale, Paris
14b Stone portrait bust of a Ptolemaic queen (Cleopatra II or III), mid-2d century BCE. Louvre, Paris
15a Alexandrian coin, showing the Serapeion. Bibliothèque Nationale, Paris
15b Jean-Alexandre Duruy, map of Ptolemaic Alexandria, adapted from *Etat du monde romain vers le temps de la fondation de l'empire*, 1853
16a Isis and Serapis,

detail of an Alexandrian votive relief, 2d century CE. Capitoline Museums, Rome
16b Modern model of the Lighthouse of Alexandria. Greco-Roman Museum, Alexandria
17 Hellenistic Tanagra-type terra-cotta figurines from Alexandria, 3d century BCE. Greco-Roman Museum, Alexandria
18a Greco-Roman terra-cotta lantern in the shape of an Alexandrian house or tower. Greco-Roman Museum, Alexandria
18–19 Detail of the *Nile Mosaic* from the Sanctuary of Fortuna, Praeneste (Palestrina), Roman, c. 100 BCE. National Archeological Museum, Palestrina
19a Detail of the *Nile Mosaic* from Praeneste (Palestrina). National Archeological Museum, Palestrina
20l Male sheawood statue, Ptolemaic period, 4th century BCE. Louvre, Paris
20c Papyrus, Chester Beatty Collection
21 Imaginative re-creation of the Library of Alexandria, after an 1880 Hungarian engraving
22 Obsidian cup decorated with Egyptian motifs in intarsia coral, lapis lazuli, malachite, and gold, Roman, undated. Museo Nazionale

Archeologico, Naples
23a A pair of oxen turning a waterwheel, detail of a fresco from a catacomb at Sakkieh, Egyptian, 1st century BCE. Greco-Roman Museum, Alexandria
23b Portrait statue of Panemerit, governor of Tanis, Egyptian, late Ptolemaic period. Louvre, Paris
24a–25 Head of Ptolemy XII (profile, full face, back). Private collection
24b The *Farnese Cup,* carved sardonyx cameo from Alexandria, Ptolemaic period, 2d–1st century BCE. Museo Nazionale Archeologico, Naples
26a Roman legionnaire. Museo della Civiltà Romana, Rome
26b Bust of Pompey, marble, Roman, 1st century BCE. Uffizi, Florence
27 Roman legionnaire (detail). Museo della Civiltà Romana, Rome
28–29 Map of Roman conquests from the 3d century BCE to 1st century CE
30 Cleopatra, bas-relief from the temple at Kom Ombo, Egyptian, Ptolemaic–Roman period, probably 1st century CE
31 Cleopatra. Museo Pio-Clementino, Vatican City
32 *Attis Dancing,* terra-cotta statuette from Myrina, second half of the 2d century BCE. Louvre, Paris

Index

Acknowledgments

The author wishes to thank C. Aziza, C. Bridonneau, P. Morin, F. de Polignac, C. Volpilhac- Auger, A. von Busekist. Project manager (France): Nathalie Palma.

Photograph Credits

Alinari, Rome 31. Alinari/Giraudon, Paris 7. Aliza Auerbach/ASAP, Paris 68–69b. All rights reserved 14–15, 20, 24a–25, 50a, 79, 106–7, 112. Archives Cahiers du Cinéma, Paris 66b. Archiv für Kunst und Geschichte, Berlin 12, 54, 78b. Artephot/Fiore, Paris 53. Artephot/Nimatallah, Paris 9, 22, 64a, 76b. Artephot/Percheron 105b. Artephot/Stierlin, Paris 30, 35, 37l. Artephot/Trela, Paris 88. Bibliothèque Nationale, Paris 14, 15a. BFI Stills, Posters and Designs, London 73, 76a, 77, 120, 125, 134, 149a, 149b, 151. Bridgeman Art Library, London front cover, 86, 90, 91, 94–95. Bridgeman/Giraudon, Paris 1, 8. British Museum, London 36l, 37r, 57r, 82b, 101, 102. Ny Carlsberg Glyptotek, Copenhagen 39c. J.-L. Charmet, Paris 21, 67r. Chuzeville, Paris 111b. Cinémathèque Française, Paris 42a, 42b, 43a, 43b, 44, 45b, 123, 126. Dagli Orti, Paris 16, 24b, 26a, 27, 45l, 56l, 75. Ecole Nationale Supérieure des Beaux-Arts, Paris 104–5. Editions A.C.R., Paris spine, 62–63, 70, 72–73a. Editions Berko, Knokke-Zoute 54, 96–97, 98–99. Editions Sarapis, Alexandria 13, 16b, 17, 18a, 23a, 34a, 58b, 59b, 69a, 71, 87, 103. Giraudon, Paris 4, 6, 26b, 32, 58–59. Michael Holford, London 78a, 81r. Louis Melancon, courtesy Archives, the Metropolitan Opera Association, New York 143. National Trust Photographic Library/Horst Kolo, London 92–93. Réunion des Musées Nationaux, Paris 5, 11, 14, 20l, 23b, 32–33, 34b–35, 36b–37b, 38, 38–39, 46–47, 50b, 56–57, 64b, 65, 74, 80a, 80b–81, 108–9. Roger-Viollet, Paris back cover, 66a, 93r, 113, 114, 119, 136, 124, 129, 122, 130, 142, 141, 139. Scala, Florence 2, 3, 18–19, 19, 41a, 55. Sotheby's, 1990 41b. Vertut, Issy-les-Moulineaux 100.

Text Credits

Athenaeus, *The Deipnosophists,* trans. by Charles Burton Gulick, Cambridge, Mass.: Harvard University Press, 1928, 1957, 1967 and William Heinemann Ltd, London. Hector Berlioz, *Cleopatra (Lyric Scene),* English translation by John Bernhoff © Belwyn Mills Publishing Corp. All Rights Reserved Used by Permission WARNER BROS. PUBLICATIONS U.S. INC., Miami, FL. 33014. Giovanni Boccaccio, *Concerning Famous Women,* trans. by Guido Guarino, Copyright © 1963 by Rutgers, The State University, New Brunswick. Bertolt Brecht, *The Threepenny Opera,* vol. 3 from The Modern Repertoire, Bloomington: Indiana University Press, 1960. Geoffrey Chaucer, *The Complete Poetical Works of Geoffrey Chaucer,* ed. by John S. P. Tatlock and Perry MacKaye, New York: Macmillan, 1912, 1940, reprinted 1967. Cicero, *Cicero's Letter to Atticus,* ed. by D. R. Shackleton Bailey, Cambridge, England: Cambridge University Press, 1967. Pierre Corneille, *Moot Plays of Corneille,* trans. by Lacy Lockert, Nashville, Tenn.: Vanderbilt University Press, 1959, reprinted by permission of the publishers and the Loeb Classical Library from Dio Cassius: *Dio's Roman History,* vols. 5, 6, 7 trans. by Earnest Cary, based on the version by Herbert Baldwin Foster, Cambridge, Mass.: Harvard University Press, 1968, 1969. John Dryden, *All for Love,* ed. by David M. Vieth, Lincoln: University of Nebraska Press, 1972. Gustave Flaubert, *Salammbo,* trans. by J. C. Chartres, New York: Dutton, 1969, Reprinted by Permission of Everyman's Library, David Campbell Publishers Ltd. Edward Morgan Forster, *Alexandria.* Copyright © 1961 by

Edith Flamarion is a researcher at the
Centre National de la Recherche Scientifique in Paris,
working chiefly in the area of 17th- and 18th-century
literature and painting, with a focus on mythic
and legendary women—Dido, Lucretia,
and, of course, Cleopatra.

For Christian, Antoine, and Juliette

Translated from the French by Alexandra Bonfante-Warren

For Harry N. Abrams, Inc.
Editor: Eve Sinaiko
Typographic designers: Elissa Ichiyasu, Tina Thompson
Cover designer: Dana Sloan
Text permissions: Barbara Lyons

Library of Congress Cataloging-in-Publication Data

Flamarion, Edith.
    Cleopatra : the life and death of a pharaoh / Edith Flamarion.
        p.   cm. — (Discoveries)
    Translated from French.
    Includes bibliographical references and index.
    ISBN 0–8109–2805–1
    1. Cleopatra, Queen of Egypt, d. 30 B.C.   2. Egypt—History
—332–30 B.C. 3. Queens—Egypt—Biography.   I. Title. II. Series:
Discoveries (New York, N.Y.)
DT92.7.F55   1997
932'.02'092—dc20
[B]   96–39007

Printed and bound in Italy by Editoriale Lloyd, Trieste
10 9 8 7 6 5 4